2024

THE ULTIMATE

TRAEGER

GRILL & SMOKER

COOKBOOK FOR BEGINNERS

Discover the Ultimate 1800 Days of Mouthwatering
BBQ Recipes and Master Wood Pellet Grilling, Flavorful
Recipes to Impress Your Friends.

FULL COLOR

Table of Contents

Introduction.. 4

Chapter 2: Basic Techniques and Recipes.................. 5

Chapter 3: Grilling Troubleshooting Tips................. 9

Chapter 4: Breakfast..12

Chapter 5: Appetizers and Snacks 27

Chapter 6: Poultry... 42

Chapter 7: Beef, Pork, Lamb...............................58

Chapter 8: Fish and Seafood...............................70

Chapter 9: Vegetarian Dishes..............................79

Chapter 10: Desserts.......................................86

Chapter 11: Long–Smoking Recipes 93

Chapter 12: Holiday Specials..............................97

Appendix: Measurement Conversion Chart..........100

Index...101

Introduction

Welcome to the world of Traeger grilling, where culinary creativity meets convenience and consistency. Traeger grills are not just any ordinary barbecue units; they are a revolution in the way we think about outdoor cooking. Utilizing a wood-pellet fuel system, these grills offer a unique set of advantages that elevate them above traditional charcoal or gas grills.

Wood-Pellet Fuel System

The heart of the Traeger grilling experience is its innovative wood-pellet fuel system. These grills use all-natural hardwood pellets that are fed into a burn pot by an auger, where they are ignited to create heat and smoke. This system allows for precise temperature control, which is crucial for both slow-smoked meats and quick-grilled delights. The use of wood pellets not only delivers consistent heat but also imparts a rich, smoky flavor to the food, enhancing the overall taste in a way that gas or charcoal cannot match.

Ease of Use and Precision Control

Traeger grills are renowned for their ease of use, making them accessible to grillers of all skill levels. With digital controllers that maintain exact temperatures, you can set your grill to the desired heat setting and trust it to manage the temperature throughout the cooking process. This means less guesswork and more perfect results every time. Whether you're smoking a brisket for hours or grilling a steak to juicy perfection, the Traeger takes the stress out of outdoor cooking.

Versatility

One of the most exciting aspects of Traeger grills is their versatility. These grills are designed to do more than just grill; they can smoke, roast, braise, and even bake. This versatility opens up a whole new range of culinary possibilities, from smoked ribs and brisket to roasted vegetables and baked pies, all on the same grill. This ability to perform multiple cooking techniques makes the Traeger a complete outdoor cooking solution.

Eco-Friendly and Healthier Cooking

Traeger grills are not only efficient but also eco-friendly. The pellets are made from compressed hardwood sawdust and are a byproduct of other wood manufacturing processes, making them a sustainable choice. Additionally, cooking with a Traeger is healthier as the food is cooked indirectly, reducing the risk of carcinogenic char. The pellets also produce less ash than traditional charcoal, simplifying cleanup and reducing waste.

Community and Support

Joining the Traeger community means more than just buying a grill; it means becoming part of a passionate group of food lovers and outdoor cooking enthusiasts. Traeger provides robust support through recipes, tips, and tricks available on their website and social media platforms. The community is always eager to share experiences, ensuring that you have plenty of inspiration for your next grilling adventure.

In summary, Traeger grills offer a superior grilling experience by combining the primal allure of cooking with fire and the modern convenience of technology. Whether you are a seasoned pitmaster or a novice griller, a Traeger grill opens up a world of culinary possibilities, making every meal a memorable event.

Chapter 2: Basic Techniques and Recipes

Preheating and Temperature Settings

Managing heat effectively on your Traeger grill is key to achieving perfect cooking results. Whether you're smoking, grilling, baking, or roasting, understanding how to control the temperature will allow you to master various recipes. Here's a guide on how to preheat your grill and manage temperature settings for different types of recipes.

1. Preheating Your Traeger Grill

Preheating is crucial to ensure your grill reaches the ideal cooking temperature and stabilizes there before you begin cooking. Here's how to do it:

- **Turn On the Grill:** Power on your Traeger grill and set it to the 'Smoke' setting initially to start the fire using the wood pellets. This setting helps to establish a base of heat and smoke.

- **Adjust to Cooking Temperature:** Once the fire is established and you see smoke, adjust the temperature to your desired cooking setting. The specific temperature will depend on what you're cooking.

- **Allow the Grill to Preheat:** Close the lid and allow the grill to preheat for about 10-15 minutes. This step is essential for the grill to reach the correct temperature and for the heat to distribute evenly.

2. Managing Temperature Settings

Different dishes require different cooking temperatures. Here's a basic guide to help you set the right temperature for various types of recipes:

- **Smoking (Low and Slow):** Set the grill between 165°F and 225°F. This range is perfect for slow-cooking meats like ribs, brisket, or pulled pork, allowing them to become tender and infused with smoky flavors over several hours.

- **Grilling (High Heat):** Temperatures between 450°F and 500°F are ideal for grilling steaks, burgers, or vegetables. High heat sears the exterior of the food quickly, creating a flavorful crust.

- **Baking:** Set the grill around 350°F to 375°F, similar to a conventional oven. This range is great for baking pizza, bread, or desserts like pies and cookies.

- **Roasting:** Use a temperature range of 325°F to 375°F for roasting meats and vegetables. This ensures that the food is cooked through and develops a rich, golden exterior.

- **Braising:** For dishes that require slow cooking in a liquid, like stews or braised ribs, set the grill between 275°F and 350°F. This range allows the food to simmer gently and become incredibly tender.

3. Tips for Temperature Management

- **Use a Meat Thermometer:** To ensure food safety and doneness, always use a meat thermometer to check the internal temperature of your meats.

- **Monitor and Adjust:** Keep an eye on the grill temperature during cooking, as external factors like wind or ambient temperature can affect it. Adjust the temperature settings if necessary to maintain consistent heat.

- **Utilize Indirect Heat:** For recipes that need longer cooking times, consider using indirect heat by placing the food away from the direct line of the fire pot. This technique helps in cooking the food evenly without burning the exterior.

By mastering these preheating and temperature management techniques, you'll be able to tackle a wide range of recipes on your Traeger grill, ensuring delicious outcomes every time.

Smoking, Grilling, Baking, Roasting on Your Traeger Grill

Understanding the versatility of your Traeger grill can enhance your cooking repertoire, allowing you to smoke, grill, bake, and roast with ease. Here's a brief tutorial on how to use each cooking method effectively on your Traeger.

1. Smoking - How to Smoke on a Traeger:

- **Set the Temperature:** For smoking, set your Traeger between 165°F and 225°F. This low temperature allows the smoke to infuse the food, giving it that classic barbecue flavor.

- **Prep Your Meat:** Apply your favorite rub or marinade. For larger cuts, consider a brine or injection for deeper flavor.

- **Use the Right Pellets:** Choose pellets that complement the flavor of your meat, such as hickory for pork or apple for chicken.

- **Slow and Low:** Place the meat on the grill and close the lid. Smoking can take several hours, depending on the size of the cut, so patience is key.

- **Check Internal Temperature:** Use a meat thermometer to ensure your meat reaches the safe internal temperature specific to each type of protein.

2. Grilling - How to Grill on a Traeger:

- **Set the Temperature:** Increase the temperature to a high heat range, typically between 450°F and 500°F, to grill meats like steaks or burgers.

- **Preheat the Grill:** Allow your grill to reach the desired temperature and let it heat for about 15 minutes to get nice grill marks.

- **Direct Heat:** For grilling, use direct heat. Place your food directly above the fire pot where the heat is most intense.

- **Flip for Perfection:** Flip your meats halfway through the cooking time to ensure an even cook and grill marks on both sides.

- **Monitor Closeness:** Keep a close eye on the grill as the high heat can cook food quickly and potentially burn it if left unattended.

3. Baking - How to Bake on a Traeger:

- **Set the Temperature:** Set your Traeger to mimic an oven, usually around 350°F to 375°F, ideal for most baking recipes.
- **Preheat the Grill:** It's crucial to let your grill come up to temperature to ensure your baked goods cook evenly.

- **Use Cookware:** For baking, you'll often need to use a dish or pan suitable for the grill, such as cast iron or any grill-safe baking dish.

- **Check Doneness:** Since every recipe is different, use a toothpick or a cake tester to check the doneness of cakes, bread, or cookies.

4. Roasting - How to Roast on a Traeger:

- **Set the Temperature:** Roasting is performed at a moderate heat, usually between 325°F and 375°F.

- **Preheat the Grill:** As with baking, ensure your grill is fully preheated to maintain a stable cooking environment.

- **Prepare Your Roast:** Season your meat or vegetables well. Use a roasting rack if available, to elevate the meat and allow heat to circulate freely.

- **Cook Evenly:** Roasting can take a few hours depending on the size of your roast. Use indirect heat for even cooking and rotate your dish halfway through to promote uniform cooking.

- **Rest Before Serving:** Allow your roast to rest before cutting into it to let the juices redistribute for optimum flavor and moisture.

By mastering these four cooking techniques, you'll unlock all the culinary potential of your Traeger grill, enabling you to create a wide array of delicious dishes right in your backyard.

Basic Recipes: Seasoning Mixes, Marinades, and Sauces

Having a few go-to recipes for seasoning mixes, marinades, and sauces can greatly enhance the flavors of your dishes cooked on the Traeger grill. Here are some foundational recipes that you can use in a variety of dishes throughout this cookbook.

1. All-Purpose BBQ Rub

Ingredients:
- 1/4 cup brown sugar
- 1/4 cup paprika
- 3 tablespoons black pepper
- 3 tablespoons coarse salt
- 1 tablespoon hickory smoked salt
- 2 teaspoons garlic powder
- 2 teaspoons onion powder
- 1 teaspoon cayenne pepper (adjust based on heat preference)

Instructions:
1. Combine all ingredients in a bowl and mix thoroughly.
2. Store in an airtight container in a cool, dry place. Use this rub for meats like pork, chicken, and beef to add a deep, smoky flavor.

2. Basic Marinade for Meat
Ingredients:
- 1/2 cup olive oil
- 1/4 cup soy sauce
- 1/4 cup apple cider vinegar
- 2 tablespoons mustard
- 2 tablespoons honey
- 3 cloves garlic, minced
- 1 teaspoon black pepper
- 1 teaspoon rosemary, finely chopped

Instructions:
1. Whisk all ingredients together in a bowl until the honey and mustard are fully incorporated.
2. Place the meat in a resealable plastic bag or shallow dish and pour the marinade over it.
3. Marinate in the refrigerator for at least 2 hours, or up to 12 hours for deeper flavor.

3. Classic BBQ Sauce
Ingredients:
- 1 cup ketchup
- 1/2 cup apple cider vinegar
- 1/3 cup brown sugar
- 1/4 cup molasses
- 1 tablespoon smoked paprika
- 1 tablespoon ground mustard
- 2 teaspoons garlic powder
- 1/2 teaspoon ground black pepper
- Hot sauce to taste

Instructions:
1. Combine all ingredients in a saucepan over medium heat.
2. Bring to a simmer and cook for 20 minutes, stirring occasionally.
3. Allow the sauce to cool. Use immediately or store in the refrigerator in an airtight container for up to 2 weeks. This sauce is perfect for brushing on ribs, chicken, or pork during the last few minutes of grilling or smoking.

4. Lemon Herb Marinade
(Great for Fish and Vegetables)
Ingredients:
- 1/3 cup olive oil
- 1/3 cup lemon juice
- 2 cloves garlic, minced
- 1 tablespoon fresh parsley, chopped
- 1 tablespoon fresh basil, chopped
- 1 teaspoon salt
- 1/2 teaspoon cracked black pepper

Instructions:
1. In a bowl, whisk together all ingredients until well combined.
2. Use this marinade for fish or fresh vegetables before grilling. Marinate fish for no more than 30 minutes to avoid overpowering the delicate flavors.

These basic recipes are versatile and can be adjusted to suit your taste preferences or specific dietary needs. They provide a solid foundation for many of the delicious dishes you'll create with your Traeger grill, enhancing flavors and ensuring moist, tender results.

Chapter 3: Grilling Troubleshooting Tips

1. Uneven Cooking

Issue: Food cooks unevenly, with some parts overcooked and others undercooked.

Solutions:
- **Preheat Properly:** Ensure the grill is fully preheated before placing food on it. This can help in even distribution of heat.
- **Use Indirect Heat:** For thicker cuts of meat, use indirect heat by placing the food away from direct flames.
- **Rotate and Flip:** Rotate and flip the food at regular intervals to ensure all sides are exposed to the heat evenly.
- **Check Hotspots:** Identify and manage hotspots by moving food around the grill to avoid burning certain areas.

2. Excessive Smoke

Issue: Too much smoke during grilling can affect the taste of the food.
Solutions:

- **Clean the Grill:** Regularly clean the grill to remove grease and food particles that can cause excessive smoke.
- **Control Airflow:** Ensure proper ventilation by adjusting the grill's vents to control airflow.
- **Use Proper Wood Pellets:** Use the recommended type of wood pellets for your grill and avoid using damp pellets which can produce more smoke.

3. Flare-Ups

Issue: Sudden bursts of flame that can char the food and create a fire hazard.
Solutions:
- **Trim Excess Fat:** Trim excess fat from meats to reduce grease drippings that cause flare-ups.
- **Use a Drip Pan:** Place a drip pan under the grill to catch grease and prevent it from causing flare-ups.
- **Monitor Closely:** Keep an eye on the grill and have a spray bottle of water handy to douse small flare-ups.

4. Food Sticking to the Grates

Issue: Food sticks to the grill grates, making it difficult to turn and often tearing the food.

Solutions:
- **Preheat and Oil the Grates:** Preheat the grill and brush the grates with oil before placing the food on them.
- **Use Non-Stick Spray:** Apply a non-stick cooking spray on the grates.
- **Proper Cleaning:** Keep the grill grates clean to prevent food from sticking to leftover residues.

5. Dry or Overcooked Food

Issue: Food turns out dry or overcooked, losing its juiciness and flavor.

Solutions:
- **Monitor Temperature:** Use a meat thermometer to ensure food is cooked to the right temperature and not overcooked.
- **Marinate:** Marinate meats to retain moisture and add flavor.
- **Rest Meat:** Let the meat rest for a few minutes after grilling to allow juices to redistribute.

6. Under-Cooked Food

Issue: Food is not cooked thoroughly, posing a health risk.

Solutions:
- **Check Internal Temperature:** Use a meat thermometer to check the internal temperature, ensuring it reaches the safe cooking temperature.
- **Increase Cooking Time:** If food is undercooked, return it to the grill and continue cooking until done.
- **Thin Out Thick Cuts:** For very thick cuts of meat, consider butterflying or slicing them thinner to reduce cooking time.

7. Temperature Control Issues

Issue: Difficulty maintaining the desired temperature on the grill.

Solutions:
- **Preheat Correctly:** Preheat the grill properly and maintain consistent fuel levels.
- **Check for Leaks:** Ensure there are no leaks in the grill that could be causing temperature fluctuations.
- **Adjust Vents:** Use the grill's vents to control the airflow and maintain a steady temperature.

8. Grill Not Igniting

Issue: The grill fails to ignite or keep a flame.

Solutions:
- **Check Fuel Supply:** Ensure you have enough fuel (propane, pellets, or charcoal) and that it is properly connected.
- **Clean Ignition Components:** Clean the ignition system and burners to ensure there is no blockage.
- **Inspect Igniter:** Check the igniter for any damage and replace if necessary.

By following these troubleshooting tips, you can address common grilling issues and ensure a smoother, more enjoyable grilling experience.

Maintenance and Safety Tips

Proper maintenance and adherence to safety guidelines are crucial for ensuring your Traeger grill operates safely and efficiently for years to come. Here are some essential tips for cleaning, maintaining, and safely using your Traeger grill.

Maintenance Tips

1. **Regular Cleaning:** After each use, clean the grill grates with a grill brush to remove food particles and prevent buildup. Regularly empty the grease trap and dispose of the grease properly to avoid fire hazards.

2. **Deep Cleaning:** Schedule a deep cleaning every few months, depending on usage. This involves removing the grill grates, heat baffle, and grease drain pan to thoroughly scrub and remove any accumulated grease and debris. Also, vacuum out the firepot to remove ash and unburned pellets, which ensures better airflow and more efficient burning.

3. **Check Pellet Quality:** Always use high-quality, dry wood pellets. Store pellets in a dry, airtight container to prevent them from absorbing moisture, which can lead to poor combustion and potential auger blockages.

4. **Inspect Components:** Regularly inspect the grill's components, such as the auger, hopper, and firepot, for signs of wear or damage. Look for any rust or corrosion and address it promptly to prevent further deterioration.

5. **Winter Care:** If you live in a cold climate, consider using an insulation blanket to help maintain temperature control during grilling. Also, covering your grill with a waterproof cover will protect it from the elements when not in use.

6. **Keep Software Updated:** If your Traeger grill has a WiFIRE controller or any other smart features, keep the software updated to ensure you have the latest functionalities and security features.

Safety Tips

1. **Placement of the Grill:** Always place your grill on a stable, level surface, away from any flammable materials such as trees, wooden decks, or buildings. There should be at least a three-foot clearance around the grill.

2. **Never Leave the Grill Unattended:** While the grill is in use, especially when set to high temperatures or when smoking for long durations, never leave it unattended.

3. **Use Heat-Resistant Gloves:** Always wear heat-resistant gloves when handling the grill grates, adjusting the vents, adding pellets, or handling hot food directly from the grill.

4. **Proper Lighting and Shutting Down:** Follow the manufacturer's instructions for lighting and shutting down the grill. Ensure the grill is completely turned off and cooled down before

covering it or storing it away.

5. **Check for Gas Leaks:** If your model uses a gas starter or you have a dual fuel model, regularly check for gas leaks using a soapy water solution. Apply it to the gas connections and hoses; bubbles forming indicate a leak that must be addressed immediately.

6. **Child and Pet Safety:** Keep children and pets away from the grill area to avoid accidental burns or other injuries.

By following these maintenance and safety tips, you will ensure that your Traeger grill remains a reliable, safe, and enjoyable tool for outdoor cooking. Regular care not only prolongs the life of your grill but also enhances your grilling experience, helping you achieve the best results every time you cook.

Essential Tools and Accessories

To make the most of your Traeger grilling experience, having the right tools and accessories can significantly enhance your cooking efficiency and enjoyment. Here's a list of essential grilling tools and some optional accessories that can take your Traeger experience to the next level:

Essential Tools

1. **Meat Thermometer:** A digital meat thermometer is crucial for ensuring your meats are cooked to the perfect temperature. It helps avoid undercooking or overcooking, providing safety and precision in your cooking.

2. **Grill Tongs:** Long-handled, durable tongs are necessary for safely turning and handling food on the grill. Look for ones with a good grip to handle food securely.

3. **Grill Brush:** Keeping your grill clean is essential for performance and longevity. A sturdy grill brush will help you clean the grates after each use, preventing buildup and ensuring even cooking.

4. **Grill Spatula:** A long-handled spatula is ideal for flipping burgers, fish, or large vegetables. Opt for a spatula with a sturdy handle and a wide base.

5. **Grilling Gloves:** High-temperature resistant gloves protect your hands from heat when managing the grill or handling hot food directly.

6. **Pellet Storage Bucket:** To keep your wood pellets dry and ready for use, a storage bucket with a tight-sealing lid is essential. This helps preserve the quality and burn efficiency of the pellets.

Optional Accessories

1. **Pellet Flavor Variety Pack:** Experiment with different flavors of Traeger wood pellets to discover the unique taste each type brings to your food, such as hickory, apple, mesquite, or cherry.

2. **Cover:** Protect your Traeger grill from the elements with a durable cover, especially if you keep your grill outdoors. This helps prevent rust and keeps the grill clean.

3. **Folding Front Shelf:** Add a folding front shelf to your grill to increase workspace for preparing food, placing tools, or resting platters.

4. **Chicken Throne:** Use a chicken throne to cook beer can chicken. It helps the chicken roast evenly while infusing it with the moisture and flavor of your choice of liquid.

5. **Rib Rack:** A rib rack maximizes the space on your grill, allowing you to cook multiple racks of ribs vertically, increasing the amount you can cook at once.

6. **Cast Iron Cookware:** Utilize cast iron griddles or pans to expand the types of dishes you can prepare on your Traeger, such as pancakes, eggs, or even artisan pizzas.

7. **Insulation Blanket:** For colder climates, an insulation blanket can help maintain a consistent temperature within your grill, making it more efficient during the winter months.

Chapter 4: Breakfast

Smoked Apple Cinnamon Oatmeal

Prep Time: 10 minutes | Cooking Time: 25 minutes | Serves: 4

Ingredients:
- 2 cups rolled oats
- 4 cups water
- 2 apples, peeled and diced
- 1/2 cup raisins
- 1/4 cup brown sugar
- 1 teaspoon cinnamon
- 1/4 teaspoon nutmeg
- 1/4 teaspoon salt
- Chopped nuts and additional cinnamon for garnish

Instructions:
1. Preheat your Traeger grill to 375°F.
2. In a cast iron skillet or heavy pot, combine all ingredients and mix well.
3. Place on the grill and close the lid. Cook for about 25 minutes, stirring occasionally, until the oats are fully cooked and the apples are tender.
4. Serve hot, garnished with chopped nuts and a sprinkle of cinnamon.

Traeger Breakfast Burgers

Prep Time: 15 minutes | Cooking Time: 30 minutes | Serves: 4

Ingredients:
- 1 lb ground sausage
- 4 eggs
- 4 slices cheddar cheese
- 4 English muffins, split and toasted
- 4 lettuce leaves
- 1 tomato, sliced
- Salt and pepper to taste

Instructions:
1. Preheat your Traeger grill to 350°F.
2. Form the sausage into 4 patties and season with salt and pepper.
3. Grill the patties for about 5-6 minutes per side or until fully cooked.
4. In the last few minutes, top each patty with a slice of cheese to melt.
5. Meanwhile, cook eggs to your preference, either directly on the grill in a skillet or using egg rings.
6. Assemble the burgers using toasted English muffins as buns, adding a lettuce leaf, tomato slice, sausage patty with cheese, and a cooked egg.
7. Serve immediately.

Smoked Salmon and Cream Cheese Bagels

Prep Time: 5 minutes | Cooking Time: 15 minutes | Serves: 4

Ingredients:
- 4 bagels, halved
- 8 oz smoked salmon
- 4 oz cream cheese, softened
- 1 red onion, thinly sliced
- Capers, for garnish
- Fresh dill, for garnish

Instructions:
1. Preheat your Traeger grill to 350°F.
2. Place bagel halves on the grill, cut side down, and toast lightly for about 5 minutes.
3. Spread each bagel half with cream cheese, then top with smoked salmon, sliced onion, and capers.
4. Garnish with fresh dill and serve.

Grilled Peach and Yogurt Parfait

Prep Time: 10 minutes | Cooking Time: 10 minutes | Serves: 4

Ingredients:
- 4 peaches, halved and pitted
- 2 cups plain Greek yogurt
- 1/4 cup honey
- 1/2 cup granola
- Mint leaves for garnish

Instructions:
1. Preheat your Traeger grill to 350°F.
2. Place peach halves on the grill, cut side down, and grill for about 5-7 minutes until they are slightly softened and have grill marks.
3. In serving bowls or glasses, layer Greek yogurt, grilled peaches (sliced), and granola.
4. Drizzle with honey and garnish with mint leaves.

Traeger Grilled French Toast

Prep Time: 10 minutes | Cooking Time: 20 minutes | Serves: 4

Ingredients:
- 8 slices of thick-cut bread (like brioche or challah)
- 4 eggs
- 1 cup milk
- 1/4 cup sugar
- 1 teaspoon vanilla extract
- 1/2 teaspoon cinnamon
- Butter for grilling
- Maple syrup and powdered sugar for serving

Instructions:
1. Preheat your Traeger grill to 350°F.
2. In a large bowl, whisk together eggs, milk, sugar, vanilla, and cinnamon.
3. Dip each bread slice into the egg mixture, ensuring both sides are well coated.
4. Butter the grill grates lightly and place the soaked bread slices on the grill.
5. Cook for about 10 minutes per side or until golden brown and cooked through.
6. Serve hot with maple syrup and a dusting of powdered sugar.

Hickory Smoked Breakfast Sausage

Prep Time: 10 minutes | Cooking Time: 20 minutes | Serves: 4

Ingredients:
- 1 lb fresh ground pork
- 1 tablespoon maple syrup
- 1 teaspoon sage, finely chopped
- 1 teaspoon thyme, finely chopped
- 1/2 teaspoon fennel seeds, crushed
- 1/2 teaspoon garlic powder
- 1/2 teaspoon salt
- 1/4 teaspoon black pepper

Instructions:
1. Preheat your Traeger grill to 275°F.
2. In a bowl, combine all ingredients thoroughly. Form the mixture into 8 small patties.
3. Place the patties on the grill and cook for about 10 minutes per side or until cooked through and slightly crispy on the outside.

Traeger Baked Blueberry Muffins

Prep Time: 15 minutes | Cooking Time: 20 minutes | Serves: 6

Ingredients:
- 2 cups all-purpose flour
- 1/2 cup sugar
- 3 teaspoons baking powder
- 1/2 teaspoon salt
- 1 cup milk
- 1/4 cup vegetable oil
- 1 large egg
- 1 cup fresh blueberries

Instructions:
1. Preheat your Traeger grill to 375°F.
2. In a large bowl, mix together flour, sugar, baking powder, and salt. In another bowl, whisk together milk, oil, and egg.
3. Combine the wet and dry ingredients until just mixed. Fold in the blueberries gently.
4. Spoon the batter into a greased muffin tin, filling each cup about two-thirds full.
5. Place the tin on the grill and bake for 20 minutes or until a toothpick inserted into the center of a muffin comes out clean.

Grilled Grapefruit with Honey and Cinnamon

Prep Time: 5 minutes | Cooking Time: 10 minutes | Serves: 4

Ingredients:
- 2 grapefruits, halved
- 4 teaspoons honey
- 1/2 teaspoon cinnamon

Instructions:
1. Preheat your Traeger grill to 350°F.
2. Sprinkle each grapefruit half with cinnamon and drizzle with honey.
3. Place grapefruit halves directly on the grill, cut side down, and grill for about 10 minutes or until the fruit is warm and slightly caramelized.

Smoked Hash Browns
Prep Time: 10 minutes | Cooking Time: 30 minutes | Serves: 4

Ingredients:
- 4 large potatoes, shredded
- 1 onion, finely chopped
- 1/4 cup cooking oil
- Salt and pepper to taste

Instructions:
1. Preheat your Traeger grill to 375°F.
2. In a bowl, mix the shredded potatoes and onion with oil, salt, and pepper.
3. Spread the potato mixture evenly on a large cast-iron skillet or grill-safe pan.
4. Place on the grill and cook for about 15 minutes per side or until golden brown and crispy.

Traeger Smoked Crepes
Prep Time: 10 minutes | Cooking Time: 20 minutes | Serves: 4

Ingredients:
- 1 cup all-purpose flour
- 2 eggs
- 1/2 cup milk
- 1/2 cup water
- 1/4 teaspoon salt
- 2 tablespoons melted butter

Instructions:
1. Preheat your Traeger grill to 375°F.
2. In a blender, combine all ingredients until smooth.
3. Lightly grease a non-stick skillet and place it on the grill. Pour about 1/4 cup of batter onto the skillet, tilting it to spread the batter evenly.
4. Cook each crepe for about 2 minutes per side or until lightly golden.
5. Serve warm with your choice of sweet or savory fillings.

Traeger Smoked Cheddar Biscuits
Prep Time: 15 minutes | Cooking Time: 20 minutes | Serves: 6

Ingredients:
- 2 cups all-purpose flour
- 1 tablespoon baking powder
- 1 teaspoon salt
- 1/2 teaspoon garlic powder
- 1 cup sharp cheddar cheese, shredded
- 1 cup buttermilk
- 1/2 cup unsalted butter, melted

Instructions:
1. Preheat your Traeger grill to 425°F.
2. In a large bowl, combine flour, baking powder, salt, and garlic powder. Stir in cheese.
3. Mix in buttermilk and melted butter until a soft dough forms.
4. Drop spoonfuls of dough onto a baking sheet lined with parchment paper.
5. Bake for 18-20 minutes or until golden brown.

Applewood Smoked Turkey Bacon
Prep Time: 5 minutes | Cooking Time: 20 minutes | Serves: 4

Ingredients:
- 1 pound turkey bacon

Instructions:
1. Preheat your Traeger grill to 300°F.
2. Arrange turkey bacon strips on the grill grate.
3. Smoke for 20 minutes or until crispy.

Grilled Avocado Boats
Prep Time: 10 minutes | Cooking Time: 15 minutes | Serves: 4

Ingredients:
- 4 avocados, halved and pitted
- 8 eggs
- Salt and pepper to taste
- Chopped chives for garnish

Instructions:
1. Preheat your Traeger grill to 350°F.
2. Crack an egg into the center of each avocado half.
3. Season with salt and pepper.
4. Grill for 15 minutes or until the eggs are set.

Smoked Salmon Frittata

Prep Time: 15 minutes | Cooking Time: 25 minutes | Serves: 6

Ingredients:
- 8 eggs
- 1/2 cup cream
- 1/2 teaspoon salt
- 1/4 teaspoon black pepper
- 1 cup smoked salmon, chopped
- 1/2 cup red onion, finely diced
- 1/4 cup capers
- 1/4 cup dill, chopped

Instructions:
1. Preheat your Traeger grill to 375°F.
2. Whisk together eggs, cream, salt, and pepper.
3. Stir in salmon, onion, capers, and dill.
4. Pour mixture into a greased baking dish.
5. Cook for 25 minutes or until eggs are set and top is lightly golden.

Blueberry Granola Crunch

Prep Time: 10 minutes | Cooking Time: 30 minutes | Serves: 4

Ingredients:
- 2 cups rolled oats
- 1/2 cup sliced almonds
- 1/2 cup honey
- 1/4 cup unsalted butter, melted
- 1 cup blueberries

Instructions:
1. Preheat your Traeger grill to 325°F.
2. In a bowl, mix oats, almonds, honey, and melted butter.
3. Spread mixture on a baking sheet and grill for 30 minutes, stirring occasionally.
4. Stir in blueberries in the last 5 minutes.

Smoked Breakfast Hash

Prep Time: 15 minutes | Cooking Time: 35 minutes | Serves: 4

Ingredients:
- 2 large potatoes, diced
- 1 red bell pepper, diced
- 1 green bell pepper, diced
- 1 onion, diced
- 1 cup cooked ham, diced
- 4 eggs
- 1/2 cup shredded cheddar cheese
- Salt and pepper to taste
- 2 tablespoons olive oil

Instructions:
1. Preheat your Traeger grill to 375°F.
2. Toss potatoes, bell peppers, onion, and ham with olive oil, salt, and pepper in a large bowl.
3. Spread the mixture onto a large cast-iron skillet and place on the grill.
4. Cook for about 30 minutes, stirring occasionally, until the potatoes are tender.
5. Make four wells in the hash and crack an egg into each.
6. Sprinkle cheese over the entire skillet and close the grill lid.
7. Cook for an additional 5 minutes or until the eggs are cooked to your liking.

Grilled Pancakes

Prep Time: 10 minutes | Cooking Time: 15 minutes | Serves: 4

Ingredients:
- 2 cups all-purpose flour
- 2 tablespoons sugar
- 2 teaspoons baking powder
- 1/2 teaspoon salt
- 2 eggs
- 1 1/2 cups milk
- 1/4 cup melted butter
- Butter or oil for greasing

Instructions:
1. Preheat your Traeger grill to 350°F.
2. In a large bowl, whisk together flour, sugar, baking powder, and salt.
3. In another bowl, beat the eggs with milk and melted butter.
4. Combine the wet ingredients with the dry ingredients and stir until smooth.
5. Grease a cast-iron skillet or flat grill plate and pour 1/4 cup of batter for each pancake.
6. Cook for about 2-3 minutes per side or until golden brown and cooked through.

Smoked Veggie Omelet

Prep Time: 10 minutes | Cooking Time: 25 minutes | Serves: 2

Ingredients:
- 4 eggs
- 1/4 cup milk
- 1/2 cup spinach, chopped
- 1/4 cup mushrooms, sliced
- 1/4 cup cherry tomatoes, halved
- 1/4 cup shredded cheese
- Salt and pepper to taste
- 1 tablespoon olive oil

Instructions:
1. Preheat your Traeger grill to 325°F.
2. In a bowl, whisk together eggs, milk, salt, and pepper.
3. Heat olive oil in a cast-iron skillet on the grill.
4. Pour in the egg mixture, then evenly distribute spinach, mushrooms, and tomatoes over the top.
5. Close the grill lid and cook for about 20 minutes, or until the eggs are set.
6. Sprinkle cheese on top, close the lid again, and cook for another 5 minutes until the cheese is melted.

Cinnamon Apple Smoked Oatmeal

Prep Time: 5 minutes | Cooking Time: 30 minutes | Serves: 4

Ingredients:
- 2 cups rolled oats
- 4 cups water or milk
- 2 apples, peeled and chopped
- 1/4 cup raisins
- 1/4 cup brown sugar
- 1 teaspoon cinnamon
- 1/4 teaspoon nutmeg

Instructions:
1. Preheat your Traeger grill to 300°F.
2. Combine all ingredients in a heatproof dish.
3. Place the dish on the grill and close the lid.
4. Cook for 30 minutes, stirring occasionally, until the oatmeal is creamy and apples are tender.

Grilled French Toast Kebabs

Prep Time: 15 minutes | Cooking Time: 10 minutes | Serves: 4

Ingredients:
- 8 thick slices of day-old bread, cubed
- 3 eggs
- 1 cup milk
- 1/4 cup sugar
- 1 teaspoon vanilla extract
- 1/2 teaspoon cinnamon
- Butter for grilling
- Maple syrup for serving

Instructions:
1. Preheat your Traeger grill to 350°F.
2. In a large bowl, whisk together eggs, milk, sugar, vanilla, and cinnamon.
3. Dip bread cubes in the egg mixture, ensuring each piece is well coated.
4. Thread the soaked bread cubes onto skewers.
5. Grease the grill grates with butter and place the skewers on the grill.
6. Cook for about 5 minutes per side or until golden brown and crispy.
7. Serve hot with maple syrup.

Smoked Breakfast Tacos

Prep Time: 20 minutes | Cooking Time: 30 minutes | Serves: 4

Ingredients:
- 8 small corn tortillas
- 6 eggs, beaten
- 1 cup chorizo sausage, cooked and crumbled
- 1/2 cup diced onions
- 1/2 cup bell peppers, diced
- 1 cup shredded Monterey Jack cheese
- 1 avocado, diced
- 1/4 cup fresh cilantro, chopped
- Salsa and sour cream for serving

Instructions:
1. Preheat your Traeger grill to 350°F.
2. In a cast iron skillet on the grill, cook the chorizo until browned. Remove and set aside.
3. In the same skillet, add onions and bell peppers, cooking until softened.
4. Pour the eggs over the vegetables, stirring gently to

combine. Cook until the eggs are set.

5. Warm the tortillas on the grill, flipping once to heat both sides.

6. Assemble the tacos by placing a scoop of the egg mixture into each tortilla, followed by chorizo, cheese, avocado, and cilantro.

7. Serve with salsa and sour cream on the side.

Grilled Banana Bread
Prep Time: 15 minutes | Cooking Time: 1 hour | Serves: 6-8

Ingredients:
- 1 cup mashed ripe bananas (about 3 medium bananas)
- 1/3 cup melted butter
- 3/4 cup sugar
- 1 egg, beaten
- 1 teaspoon vanilla extract
- 1 teaspoon baking soda
- Pinch of salt
- 1 1/2 cups all-purpose flour
- 1/2 cup chopped walnuts

Instructions:
1. Preheat your Traeger grill to 325°F.
2. In a large bowl, mix mashed bananas with melted butter. Stir in sugar, egg, and vanilla.
3. Mix in baking soda and salt. Add flour and mix until just incorporated. Fold in nuts if using.
4. Pour the batter into a greased loaf pan.
5. Place the pan on the grill and bake for about 60 minutes or until a toothpick inserted into the center comes out clean.

Smoked Shakshuka
Prep Time: 10 minutes | Cooking Time: 45 minutes | Serves: 4

Ingredients:
- 1 tablespoon olive oil
- 1 onion, diced
- 1 red bell pepper, diced
- 2 garlic cloves, minced
- 2 cups tomato sauce
- 1 teaspoon cumin
- 1 teaspoon paprika
- 1/2 teaspoon chili powder
- Salt and pepper to taste
- 4 eggs
- Fresh parsley for garnish

Instructions:
1. Preheat your Traeger grill to 375°F.
2. In a cast-iron skillet on the grill, heat olive oil. Add onion and bell pepper, and sauté until softened.
3. Add garlic, sauté for another minute.
4. Stir in tomato sauce and spices. Simmer for about 10 minutes to allow flavors to meld.
5. Make four indentations in the sauce and crack an egg into each.
6. Close the grill lid and cook until eggs are set, about 15 minutes.
7. Garnish with parsley before serving.

Grilled Peaches and Cream French Toast
Prep Time: 20 minutes | Cooking Time: 20 minutes | Serves: 4

Ingredients:
- 8 slices of thick brioche bread
- 4 eggs
- 1 cup milk
- 1 teaspoon vanilla extract
- 1/2 teaspoon cinnamon
- 4 peaches, halved and pitted
- Cream cheese, softened
- Maple syrup for serving

Instructions:
1. Preheat your Traeger grill to 350°F.
2. In a large bowl, whisk together eggs, milk, vanilla, and cinnamon.
3. Dip each slice of bread into the egg mixture, coating both sides.
4. Grill the bread on each side until golden brown, about 3-4 minutes per side.
5. Grill the peaches cut side down until they are warm and have grill marks, about 5 minutes.
6. Spread a layer of cream cheese on each slice of French toast, top with grilled peaches, and drizzle with maple syrup.

Smoked Salmon and Asparagus Frittata

Prep Time: 10 minutes | Cooking Time: 25 minutes | Serves: 4

Ingredients:
- 6 eggs
- 1/4 cup milk
- Salt and pepper to taste
- 1 cup smoked salmon, chopped
- 1 cup asparagus, trimmed and cut into 1-inch pieces
- 1/2 cup diced onions
- 1/2 cup grated Parmesan cheese

Instructions:
1. Preheat your Traeger grill to 375°F.
2. In a large bowl, whisk together eggs, milk, salt, and pepper.
3. Stir in salmon, asparagus, onions, and half of the Parmesan cheese.
4. Pour the mixture into a greased cast-iron skillet.
5. Sprinkle the remaining cheese on top.
6. Place the skillet on the grill and cook for about 25 minutes or until the eggs are set and the top is lightly golden.

Traeger Smoked Cheese Grits

Prep Time: 10 minutes | Cooking Time: 40 minutes | Serves: 4

Ingredients:
- 1 cup grits
- 4 cups water
- 1 teaspoon salt
- 1 cup sharp cheddar cheese, shredded
- 1/4 cup Parmesan cheese, grated
- 1/2 cup cream
- 2 tablespoons butter
- 1/2 teaspoon black pepper

Instructions:
1. Preheat your Traeger grill to 350°F.
2. In a medium pot, bring water and salt to a boil. Slowly whisk in the grits.
3. Reduce heat to low, cover, and cook for 30-35 minutes, stirring occasionally, until grits are thick and creamy.
4. Stir in the cheddar cheese, Parmesan, cream, butter, and black pepper until well combined.
5. Pour the grits into a greased baking dish and grill for

an additional 10 minutes until hot and bubbly.

Grilled French Croissant Sandwich

Prep Time: 10 minutes | Cooking Time: 5 minutes | Serves: 4

Ingredients:
- 4 croissants, halved
- 8 slices of cooked ham
- 4 eggs, fried
- 4 slices Swiss cheese
- 1 avocado, sliced
- Mayonnaise and mustard for spreading

Instructions:
1. Preheat your Traeger grill to 350°F.
2. Spread mayonnaise and mustard on each half of the croissants.
3. Layer ham, a fried egg, Swiss cheese, and avocado slices on the bottom half of each croissant.
4. Place the assembled sandwiches on the grill, cover with the top halves of the croissants, and close the grill lid.
5. Grill for about 5 minutes or until the cheese is melted and the croissant is toasted.

Smoked Maple Bacon Muffins

Prep Time: 15 minutes | Cooking Time: 20 minutes | Serves: 6

Ingredients:
- 2 cups all-purpose flour
- 1 tablespoon baking powder
- 1/2 teaspoon salt
- 1/2 cup sugar
- 1 cup milk
- 1/4 cup vegetable oil
- 1 egg
- 1/2 cup bacon, cooked and crumbled
- 1/4 cup maple syrup

Instructions:
1. Preheat your Traeger grill to 350°F.
2. In a large bowl, combine flour, baking powder, salt, and sugar.
3. In another bowl, mix together milk, oil, and egg.
4. Stir the wet ingredients into the dry ingredients until just combined. Fold in the bacon.
5. Divide the batter among 6 muffin cups and drizzle

each with maple syrup.

6. Place the muffin tin on the grill and bake for 20 minutes or until a toothpick comes out clean.

Avocado and Egg Boats

Prep Time: 5 minutes | Cooking Time: 15 minutes | Serves: 4

Ingredients:
- 4 avocados, halved and pitted
- 8 eggs
- Salt and pepper to taste
- Chopped chives for garnish

Instructions:
1. Preheat your Traeger grill to 350°F.
2. Crack an egg into each avocado half, season with salt and pepper, and place on a baking sheet.
3. Grill for about 15 minutes or until the egg whites are set and the yolks are done to your liking.
4. Garnish with chopped chives before serving.

Pancetta and Vegetable Frittata

Prep Time: 20 minutes | Cooking Time: 30 minutes | Serves: 6

Ingredients:
- 8 eggs
- 1/2 cup cream
- Salt and pepper to taste
- 1 cup pancetta, diced and cooked until crispy
- 1 cup diced bell peppers
- 1/2 cup diced onions
- 1/2 cup grated cheese (your choice)
- 2 tablespoons olive oil

Instructions:
1. Preheat your Traeger grill to 375°F.
2. In a large bowl, whisk together eggs, cream, salt, and pepper.
3. Heat olive oil in a cast-iron skillet on the grill. Sauté onions and bell peppers until soft.
4. Add the cooked pancetta to the skillet and pour the egg mixture over it. Sprinkle with cheese.
5. Close the grill lid and cook for about 30 minutes or until the frittata is set.

Smoked Porridge with Mixed Berries

Prep Time: 5 minutes | Cooking Time: 30 minutes | Serves: 4

Ingredients:
- 2 cups steel-cut oats
- 4 cups water
- 1 cup mixed berries (blueberries, raspberries, strawberries)
- 1/4 cup honey
- 1 teaspoon vanilla extract
- 1/2 teaspoon cinnamon
- Milk or yogurt, for serving

Instructions:
1. Preheat your Traeger grill to 300°F.
2. Combine oats and water in a heatproof dish suitable for the grill.
3. Place the dish on the grill and cook for about 30 minutes, stirring occasionally, until the oats are tender and creamy.
4. Stir in the mixed berries, honey, vanilla, and cinnamon.
5. Serve hot with a splash of milk or a dollop of yogurt.

Grilled Tomato and Spinach Benedict

Prep Time: 15 minutes | Cooking Time: 10 minutes | Serves: 4

Ingredients:
- 4 English muffins, split
- 8 eggs
- 2 tomatoes, sliced
- 1 cup fresh spinach
- Hollandaise sauce, prepared
- Salt and pepper to taste

Instructions:
1. Preheat your Traeger grill to 350°F.
2. Grill the tomato slices for about 2 minutes on each side until just softened.
3. Poach eggs to your liking using a pan on the grill or a traditional method.
4. Toast the English muffins on the grill until lightly browned.
5. Assemble the Benedicts by layering spinach and grilled tomatoes on each muffin half, topping with a poached egg, and drizzling with Hollandaise sauce.
6. Season with salt and pepper to taste.

Smoky Bacon and Corn Pancakes

Prep Time: 10 minutes | Cooking Time: 20 minutes | Serves: 4

Ingredients:
- 1 cup all-purpose flour
- 1 tablespoon sugar
- 1 teaspoon baking powder
- 1/2 teaspoon salt
- 1 cup milk
- 1 egg
- 2 tablespoons melted butter
- 1/2 cup corn kernels (fresh or thawed if frozen)
- 4 strips bacon, cooked and crumbled

Instructions:
1. Preheat your Traeger grill to 375°F.
2. In a bowl, combine flour, sugar, baking powder, and salt.
3. In another bowl, whisk together milk, egg, and melted butter.
4. Mix the wet ingredients into the dry ingredients until just combined. Fold in corn kernels and crumbled bacon.
5. Pour 1/4 cup batter for each pancake onto a hot, lightly greased griddle or skillet placed on the grill.
6. Cook for about 3-4 minutes on each side until golden brown.

Grilled Sausage and Vegetable Hash

Prep Time: 15 minutes | Cooking Time: 25 minutes | Serves: 4

Ingredients:
- 1 pound breakfast sausage, removed from casings
- 2 potatoes, diced
- 1 bell pepper, diced
- 1 onion, diced
- 1 zucchini, diced
- Salt and pepper to taste
- 4 eggs (optional)

Instructions:
1. Preheat your Traeger grill to 375°F.
2. In a large cast-iron skillet on the grill, cook the sausage until browned and crumbly.
3. Add potatoes, bell pepper, onion, and zucchini to the skillet. Season with salt and pepper.
4. Cook for about 20 minutes, stirring occasionally, until vegetables are tender and slightly charred.
5. If desired, make four wells in the hash and crack an egg into each. Cook until the eggs are set.

Apple and Pecan Smoked Oat Crumble

Prep Time: 10 minutes | Cooking Time: 40 minutes | Serves: 4

Ingredients:
- 3 apples, peeled, cored, and sliced
- 1 cup rolled oats
- 1/2 cup flour
- 1/2 cup brown sugar
- 1/2 cup pecans, chopped
- 1/2 cup unsalted butter, cold and cubed
- 1 teaspoon cinnamon
- 1/2 teaspoon nutmeg

Instructions:
1. Preheat your Traeger grill to 350°F.
2. Arrange apple slices in a baking dish suitable for the grill.
3. In a bowl, mix oats, flour, brown sugar, pecans, cinnamon, and nutmeg. Add butter and rub into the dry ingredients until the mixture resembles coarse crumbs.
4. Sprinkle the oat mixture over the apples.
5. Place the dish on the grill and cook for about 40 minutes, or until the topping is golden and the apples are tender.

Yogurt Parfaits

Prep Time: 5 minutes | Cooking Time: 15 minutes | Serves: 4

Ingredients:
- 2 cups plain Greek yogurt
- 1/4 cup honey
- 1 teaspoon vanilla extract
- 1 cup granola
- 1 cup mixed berries (strawberries, blueberries, raspberries)
- 1/2 cup sliced almonds

Instructions:
1. Preheat your Traeger grill to 225°F.
2. In a bowl, mix yogurt with honey and vanilla extract.
3. Place the yogurt mixture in a shallow dish and

smoke on the grill for 15 minutes to infuse a subtle smoky flavor.

4. Assemble the parfaits by layering the smoked yogurt, granola, mixed berries, and almonds in serving glasses.

Hash Brown Casserole

Prep Time: 20 minutes | Cooking Time: 1 hour | Serves: 6

Ingredients:
- 1 package (30 ounces) frozen hash browns, thawed
- 1 cup sour cream
- 1 can (10.5 ounces) cream of chicken soup
- 2 cups shredded cheddar cheese
- 1/2 cup melted butter
- 1/2 cup chopped onions
- 2 cloves garlic, minced
- 1/2 teaspoon salt
- 1/4 teaspoon black pepper
- 1/2 cup crushed cornflakes or breadcrumbs for topping

Instructions:
1. Preheat your Traeger grill to 350°F.
2. In a large bowl, mix together hash browns, sour cream, cream of chicken soup, cheddar cheese, melted butter, onions, garlic, salt, and pepper.
3. Transfer the mixture to a greased baking dish.
4. Sprinkle crushed cornflakes or breadcrumbs over the top.
5. Bake on the grill for 60 minutes, or until the casserole is bubbly and golden brown on top.

Grilled Breakfast Pizzas

Prep Time: 15 minutes | Cooking Time: 10 minutes | Serves: 4

Ingredients:
- 4 pre-made individual pizza crusts
- 1/2 cup tomato sauce
- 1 cup mozzarella cheese, shredded
- 4 eggs
- 1/2 cup cooked bacon, crumbled
- 1/2 cup bell peppers, diced
- Fresh basil leaves for garnish

Instructions:
1. Preheat your Traeger grill to 400°F.
2. Spread tomato sauce on each pizza crust.

3. Sprinkle mozzarella cheese, bacon, and bell peppers over the sauce.
4. Carefully crack an egg onto the center of each pizza.
5. Grill for about 10 minutes, or until the crust is crispy and the egg whites are set.

Smoked Apple Cinnamon Rolls

Prep Time: 30 minutes | Cooking Time: 30 minutes | Serves: 12 rolls

Ingredients:
- 1 batch of your favorite cinnamon roll dough
- 2 apples, peeled and finely chopped
- 1 cup brown sugar
- 2 tablespoons cinnamon
- 1/2 cup butter, softened
- Cream cheese icing for topping

Instructions:
1. Prepare your cinnamon roll dough according to the recipe's instructions.
2. Roll out the dough into a rectangle. Spread softened butter over the dough.
3. Mix brown sugar and cinnamon together, and sprinkle it over the buttered dough. Distribute the chopped apples evenly.
4. Roll the dough tightly from the long end and cut into 12 equal slices.
5. Preheat your Traeger grill to 375°F.
6. Place the cinnamon rolls in a baking dish and let rise for 30 minutes.
7. Bake for 30 minutes or until golden brown.
8. Drizzle with cream cheese icing while still warm.

Smoky Chorizo and Egg Breakfast Burritos

Prep Time: 15 minutes | Cooking Time: 20 minutes | Serves: 4

Ingredients:
- 4 large flour tortillas
- 8 eggs, beaten
- 1 pound chorizo sausage, cooked and crumbled
- 1 cup shredded pepper jack cheese
- 1 avocado, sliced
- 1/4 cup chopped cilantro
- Salsa and sour cream for serving

Instructions:
1. Preheat your Traeger grill to 350°F.
2. Scramble the eggs on a skillet over the grill, stirring

in the cooked chorizo once the eggs begin to set.

3. Warm the tortillas on the grill for about 1 minute on each side.

4. Assemble the burritos by placing a scoop of the chorizo and egg mixture on each tortilla, topping with cheese, avocado slices, and cilantro.

5. Roll up the tortillas, tucking in the ends, and grill seam-side down for about 2 minutes, or until golden and crisp.

6. Serve with salsa and sour cream.

Smoked French Toast Sticks

Prep Time: 10 minutes | Cooking Time: 20 minutes | Serves: 4

Ingredients:
- 8 slices of thick brioche or Texas toast
- 3 eggs
- 1 cup whole milk
- 1 teaspoon vanilla extract
- 1 teaspoon ground cinnamon
- 1/4 cup granulated sugar
- Maple syrup for serving
- Powdered sugar for dusting

Instructions:
1. Preheat your Traeger grill to 350°F.
2. Cut each slice of bread into four strips.
3. In a mixing bowl, whisk together eggs, milk, vanilla, cinnamon, and granulated sugar.
4. Dip each bread strip into the egg mixture, ensuring each piece is well coated.
5. Place the bread strips on a greased wire rack on the grill.
6. Grill for about 10 minutes on each side, or until golden brown and slightly crispy.
7. Serve warm, drizzled with maple syrup and a dusting of powdered sugar.

Grilled Vegetable and Goat Cheese Frittata

Prep Time: 15 minutes | Cooking Time: 25 minutes | Serves: 6

Ingredients:
- 8 eggs
- 1/2 cup milk
- Salt and pepper to taste
- 1 zucchini, sliced
- 1 red bell pepper, chopped
- 1 small red onion, sliced
- 4 ounces goat cheese, crumbled
- 2 tablespoons olive oil
- Fresh herbs (such as basil or thyme), for garnish

Instructions:
1. Preheat your Traeger grill to 375°F.
2. In a large bowl, whisk together eggs, milk, salt, and pepper.
3. Heat olive oil in a cast iron skillet on the grill. Add zucchini, bell pepper, and onion. Cook until softened.
4. Pour the egg mixture over the vegetables in the skillet. Dot the surface with crumbled goat cheese.
5. Close the grill lid and cook for about 25 minutes, or until the eggs are set and the top is lightly golden.
6. Garnish with fresh herbs before serving.

Smoked Salmon Bagel Platter

Prep Time: 10 minutes | Cooking Time: 5 minutes | Serves: 4

Ingredients:
- 4 bagels, sliced and toasted
- 8 ounces smoked salmon
- 1/2 cup cream cheese, softened
- 1/4 red onion, thinly sliced
- 1/4 cup capers
- Fresh dill, for garnish
- Lemon wedges, for serving

Instructions:
1. Preheat your Traeger grill to 300°F.
2. Lightly toast the sliced bagels on the grill for about 2-3 minutes, until just warm and slightly crisp.
3. Spread each bagel half with cream cheese. Top with smoked salmon, sliced red onion, and capers.
4. Garnish with fresh dill and serve with lemon wedges on the side.

Peach and Ricotta Grilled Toast

Prep Time: 5 minutes | Cooking Time: 10 minutes | Serves: 4

Ingredients:
- 4 slices of sourdough bread
- 1 cup ricotta cheese
- 2 peaches, sliced
- Honey, for drizzling

- Fresh mint, for garnish

Instructions:
1. Preheat your Traeger grill to 350°F.
2. Grill the sourdough slices until toasted, about 2-3 minutes per side.
3. Spread each slice generously with ricotta cheese.
4. Top with fresh peach slices and a drizzle of honey.
5. Garnish with mint leaves and serve immediately.

Barbecue Pulled Pork Breakfast Tacos
Prep Time: 20 minutes | Cooking Time: Pork preparation | Serves: 4

Ingredients:
- Leftover pulled pork
- 8 small corn tortillas
- 4 eggs, scrambled
- 1/2 cup shredded cheddar cheese
- 1/4 cup chopped green onions
- Salsa and sour cream for serving

Instructions:
1. Reheat leftover pulled pork on the grill if not already warm.
2. Warm the tortillas on the grill, about 1 minute on each side.
3. Assemble the tacos by placing a scoop of scrambled eggs on each tortilla, followed by pulled pork.
4. Sprinkle with cheddar cheese and green onions.
5. Serve with salsa and sour cream on the side.

Smoked Coconut Porridge
Prep Time: 5 minutes | Cooking Time: 30 minutes | Serves: 4

Ingredients:
- 2 cups rolled oats
- 1 can (13.5 oz) coconut milk
- 2 cups water
- 1/4 cup shredded coconut
- 1/4 cup honey
- 1 teaspoon vanilla extract
- Pinch of salt
- Fresh mango and toasted coconut flakes, for topping

Instructions:
1. Preheat your Traeger grill to 250°F.
2. In a large pot, mix oats, coconut milk, water,

shredded coconut, honey, vanilla, and salt.
3. Place the pot on the grill and close the lid.
4. Cook for about 30 minutes, stirring occasionally, until the porridge is creamy.
5. Serve hot, topped with fresh mango slices and toasted coconut flakes.

Grilled Sweet Potato and Kale Hash
Prep Time: 15 minutes | Cooking Time: 25 minutes | Serves: 4

Ingredients:
- 2 large sweet potatoes, diced
- 1 bunch kale, stems removed and leaves chopped
- 1 red onion, diced
- 2 cloves garlic, minced
- 4 eggs
- 1/4 cup olive oil
- Salt and pepper to taste
- Smoked paprika, for sprinkling

Instructions:
1. Preheat your Traeger grill to 375°F.
2. Toss sweet potatoes, onion, and garlic with olive oil, salt, and pepper.
3. Spread the mixture in a large cast iron skillet and place on the grill.
4. Cook for about 20 minutes, stirring occasionally, until sweet potatoes are almost tender.
5. Stir in the kale and continue cooking until wilted, about 5 more minutes.
6. Make four wells in the hash and crack an egg into each.
7. Close the grill lid and cook until the eggs are set to your liking.
8. Sprinkle with smoked paprika before serving.

Smoked Cheese and Bacon Scones
Prep Time: 15 minutes | Cooking Time: 20 minutes | Serves: 8

Ingredients:
- 2 cups all-purpose flour
- 1 tablespoon baking powder
- 1/2 teaspoon salt
- 1/4 teaspoon black pepper
- 1/2 cup cold butter, cubed
- 3/4 cup milk
- 1 cup shredded smoked cheese (like Gouda or

Cheddar)
- 1/2 cup cooked bacon, chopped
- 1 egg, beaten, for brushing

Instructions:
1. Preheat your Traeger grill to 400°F.
2. In a large bowl, combine flour, baking powder, salt, and pepper.
3. Cut in the butter until the mixture resembles coarse crumbs.
4. Stir in milk, smoked cheese, and bacon until just combined.
5. Turn the dough out onto a floured surface and knead lightly.
6. Roll out to 1-inch thickness and cut into rounds with a biscuit cutter.
7. Place scones on a baking sheet, brush with beaten egg, and grill for about 20 minutes, or until golden and risen.
8. Serve warm.

Grilled Avocado with Egg and Chorizo
Prep Time: 10 minutes | Cooking Time: 15 minutes | Serves: 4

Ingredients:
- 4 avocados, halved and pitted
- 4 eggs
- 1/2 cup cooked chorizo
- Salt and pepper to taste
- Fresh cilantro, for garnish

Instructions:
1. Preheat your Traeger grill to 350°F.
2. Scoop a little extra flesh out of each avocado half to make room for an egg.
3. Place avocado halves on a grill-safe tray. Carefully crack an egg into each avocado half.
4. Season with salt and pepper, and sprinkle cooked chorizo around the eggs.
5. Grill for about 15 minutes or until the eggs are cooked to your desired doneness.
6. Garnish with fresh cilantro and serve immediately.

Smoked Berry French Toast Casserole
Prep Time: 20 minutes | Cooking Time: 45 minutes | Serves: 6
Ingredients:
- 1 loaf French bread, cut into cubes

- 8 eggs
- 2 cups milk
- 1/2 cup heavy cream
- 1/4 cup sugar
- 1 teaspoon vanilla extract
- 1 teaspoon cinnamon
- 2 cups mixed berries
- Powdered sugar, for dusting

Instructions:
1. The night before, place bread cubes in a large greased baking dish.
2. In a bowl, whisk together eggs, milk, cream, sugar, vanilla, and cinnamon.
3. Pour the egg mixture over the bread, pressing down to ensure all bread is soaked. Cover and refrigerate overnight.
4. Preheat your Traeger grill to 375°F.
5. Scatter mixed berries over the top of the soaked bread.
6. Place the casserole on the grill and cook for about 45 minutes, or until set and golden on top.
7. Dust with powdered sugar before serving.

Smoked Berry Oatmeal Crisp
Prep Time: 10 minutes | Cooking Time: 30 minutes | Serves: 4

Ingredients:
- 2 cups rolled oats
- 1 cup mixed berries (fresh or frozen)
- 1/2 cup brown sugar
- 1/4 cup flour
- 1/4 cup butter, melted
- 1/2 teaspoon cinnamon
- 1/4 teaspoon nutmeg
- 1/4 teaspoon salt

Instructions:
1. Preheat your Traeger grill to 350°F.
2. In a bowl, mix together oats, brown sugar, flour, melted butter, cinnamon, nutmeg, and salt until crumbly.
3. Place the berries in a grill-safe baking dish and sprinkle the oat mixture over the top.
4. Grill for about 30 minutes, or until the topping is golden brown and the berries are bubbly.
5. Serve warm, ideally with a dollop of yogurt or whipped cream.

Grilled Prosciutto-Wrapped Asparagus and Egg

Prep Time: 10 minutes | Cooking Time: 15 minutes | Serves: 4

Ingredients:
- 16 asparagus spears, trimmed
- 8 slices prosciutto
- 4 eggs
- Olive oil
- Salt and pepper to taste

Instructions:
1. Preheat your Traeger grill to 400°F.
2. Wrap each pair of asparagus spears with a slice of prosciutto.
3. Lightly oil the wrapped asparagus and season with salt and pepper.
4. Grill for about 10 minutes, turning occasionally, until the prosciutto is crispy.
5. Meanwhile, fry eggs to your preference in a skillet on the grill.
6. Serve each egg with a side of grilled prosciutto-wrapped asparagus.

Smoky Breakfast Pizza

Prep Time: 15 minutes | Cooking Time: 15 minutes | Serves: 4

Ingredients:
- 1 pre-made pizza dough
- 1/2 cup pizza sauce
- 1 cup shredded mozzarella cheese
- 1/2 cup cooked bacon, chopped
- 1/2 cup breakfast sausage, cooked and crumbled
- 4 eggs
- Salt and pepper to taste

Instructions:
1. Preheat your Traeger grill to 400°F.
2. Roll out the pizza dough and place it on a pizza stone or directly on the grill grates.
3. Spread the pizza sauce over the dough, then sprinkle with mozzarella, bacon, and sausage.
4. Carefully crack the eggs onto the pizza, spacing them evenly.
5. Grill for about 15 minutes, or until the crust is golden and the eggs are cooked to your liking.
6. Season with salt and pepper before serving.

Grilled Peaches and Cream Oatmeal

Prep Time: 5 minutes | Cooking Time: 20 minutes | Serves: 4

Ingredients:
- 2 cups rolled oats
- 4 cups water or milk
- 2 fresh peaches, sliced
- 1/2 cup heavy cream
- 1/4 cup honey
- 1/2 teaspoon cinnamon

Instructions:
1. Preheat your Traeger grill to 350°F.
2. Cook oats in water or milk according to package instructions in a pot on the grill.
3. In a separate skillet, grill peach slices for about 2-3 minutes on each side until caramelized.
4. Stir honey and cinnamon into the cooked oatmeal.
5. Serve oatmeal topped with grilled peaches and a drizzle of cream.

Smoked Salmon and Cream Cheese Frittata

Prep Time: 10 minutes | Cooking Time: 25 minutes | Serves: 4

Ingredients:
- 8 eggs
- 1/4 cup milk
- 4 ounces smoked salmon, chopped
- 1/4 cup cream cheese, in small dollops
- 2 tablespoons chopped dill
- Salt and pepper to taste

Instructions:
1. Preheat your Traeger grill to 325°F.
2. In a bowl, whisk together eggs, milk, salt, and pepper.
3. Pour egg mixture into a greased cast-iron skillet on the grill.
4. Add smoked salmon, dollops of cream cheese, and dill evenly over the top.
5. Close the grill lid and cook for about 25 minutes or until the eggs are set.
6. Slice and serve while warm.

Chapter 5: Appetizers and Snacks

Smoked Stuffed Jalapeños

Prep Time: 15 minutes | Cooking Time: 25 minutes | Serves: 6

Ingredients:
- 12 jalapeño peppers, halved and seeded
- 1 cup cream cheese, softened
- 1/2 cup shredded cheddar cheese
- 1/4 cup chopped green onions
- 1/2 teaspoon garlic powder
- 12 slices of bacon, cut in half

Instructions:
1. Preheat your Traeger grill to 225°F.
2. In a bowl, mix together cream cheese, cheddar cheese, green onions, and garlic powder.
3. Stuff each jalapeño half with the cheese mixture.
4. Wrap each stuffed jalapeño with a half slice of bacon, securing with a toothpick if necessary.
5. Place the jalapeños on the grill and smoke for about 25 minutes or until the bacon is crispy and the peppers are tender.

Shrimp Skewers with Lemon Garlic Butter

Prep Time: 10 minutes | Cooking Time: 10 minutes | Serves: 4

Ingredients:
- 1 pound large shrimp, peeled and deveined
- 1/4 cup butter, melted
- 2 cloves garlic, minced
- Juice of 1 lemon
- Salt and pepper to taste
- Fresh parsley, chopped for garnish

Instructions:
1. Preheat your Traeger grill to 350°F.
2. In a small bowl, mix together melted butter, garlic, lemon juice, salt, and pepper.
3. Thread shrimp onto skewers.
4. Grill the shrimp skewers for about 2-3 minutes per side, basting frequently with the lemon garlic butter.
5. Once cooked, garnish with chopped parsley and serve immediately.

Smoked Gouda and Mushroom Crostini

Prep Time: 15 minutes | Cooking Time: 10 minutes | Serves: 8

Ingredients:
- 1 baguette, sliced into 1/2-inch pieces
- 1/4 cup olive oil
- 1 cup sliced mushrooms
- 1 clove garlic, minced
- 1 cup smoked gouda cheese, grated
- Fresh thyme leaves for garnish

Instructions:
1. Preheat your Traeger grill to 375°F.
2. Brush each slice of baguette with olive oil and grill until toasted, about 1-2 minutes per side.
3. In a skillet over the grill, sauté mushrooms and garlic until tender.
4. Top each crostini with sautéed mushrooms and a generous amount of smoked gouda.
5. Return the crostini to the grill and cook until the cheese is melted.
6. Garnish with thyme leaves before serving.

Grilled Corn and Avocado Salsa

Prep Time: 10 minutes | Cooking Time: 15 minutes | Serves: 6

Ingredients:
- 4 ears of corn, husks removed
- 2 avocados, diced
- 1/2 red onion, finely chopped
- 1 jalapeño, seeded and finely chopped
- Juice of 2 limes
- 1/4 cup chopped cilantro
- Salt and pepper to taste

Instructions:
1. Preheat your Traeger grill to 400°F.
2. Grill the corn for about 10-15 minutes, turning occasionally, until charred and tender.
3. Once cooled, cut the kernels off the cob and mix with diced avocados, red onion, jalapeño, lime juice, and cilantro.
4. Season with salt and pepper and serve with tortilla chips.

Grilled Parmesan Garlic Artichokes

Prep Time: 10 minutes | Cooking Time: 20 minutes | Serves: 4

Ingredients:
- 2 artichokes, halved and choke removed
- 1/4 cup olive oil
- 2 cloves garlic, minced
- 1/4 cup grated Parmesan cheese
- Salt and pepper to taste
- Lemon wedges for serving

Instructions:
1. Preheat your Traeger grill to 375°F.
2. Brush the artichoke halves with olive oil and sprinkle with minced garlic, Parmesan, salt, and pepper.
3. Place the artichokes cut side down on the grill and cook for about 10 minutes.
4. Flip the artichokes, and continue to grill for another 10 minutes or until tender.
5. Serve warm with lemon wedges on the side.

Smoked Deviled Eggs

Prep Time: 10 minutes | Cooking Time: 30 minutes | Serves: 24 halves

Ingredients:
- 12 eggs
- 1/2 cup mayonnaise
- 1 teaspoon mustard
- 1 teaspoon apple cider vinegar
- 1/4 teaspoon paprika, plus extra for garnish
- Salt and pepper to taste
- Fresh chives, chopped for garnish

Instructions:
1. Preheat your Traeger grill to 225°F.
2. Place eggs directly on the grill grates and smoke for 30 minutes.
3. Remove eggs and immediately place in an ice bath to cool.
4. Once cooled, peel the eggs and halve them lengthwise.
5. Remove the yolks and mix them with mayonnaise, mustard, vinegar, paprika, salt, and pepper until smooth.
6. Pipe or spoon the yolk mixture back into the egg whites.
7. Sprinkle with additional paprika and garnish with chopped chives before serving.

Grilled Brie with Honey and Pecans

Prep Time: 5 minutes | Cooking Time: 10 minutes | Serves: 4

Ingredients:
- 1 wheel of Brie cheese
- 1/4 cup honey
- 1/4 cup chopped pecans
- Crackers or sliced baguette, for serving

Instructions:
1. Preheat your Traeger grill to 350°F.
2. Place the Brie on a small, grill-safe pan or platter.
3. Grill for about 10 minutes or until the Brie starts to soften and melt.
4. Drizzle honey over the Brie and sprinkle with chopped pecans.
5. Serve immediately with crackers or slices of baguette for dipping.

Smoky Grilled Guacamole

Prep Time: 15 minutes | Cooking Time: 5 minutes | Serves: 6

Ingredients:
- 3 ripe avocados, halved and pitted
- 1 lime, halved
- 1 small onion, quartered
- 1 jalapeño, halved and seeded
- 1 tomato, halved
- 1/4 cup fresh cilantro, chopped
- Salt and pepper to taste

Instructions:
1. Preheat your Traeger grill to 400°F.
2. Place avocados, lime, onion, jalapeño, and tomato on the grill, cut side down.
3. Grill for about 5 minutes or until they have nice grill marks.
4. Scoop the avocado flesh into a bowl and squeeze the grilled lime over it.
5. Chop the grilled onion, jalapeño, and tomato and add to the bowl.
6. Mash the ingredients together and stir in cilantro. Season with salt and pepper.
7. Serve with tortilla chips.

Charred Edamame

Prep Time: 5 minutes | Cooking Time: 10 minutes | Serves: 4

Ingredients:
- 2 cups frozen edamame in the pod
- 2 tablespoons olive oil
- 1 teaspoon sea salt
- 1 teaspoon chili flakes
- 1 lemon, zested

Instructions:
1. Preheat your Traeger grill to 375°F.
2. Toss the edamame with olive oil, sea salt, and chili flakes.
3. Grill for about 10 minutes, turning occasionally until the pods are charred and crispy.
4. Sprinkle with lemon zest before serving.

Grilled Prosciutto-Wrapped Pears

Prep Time: 10 minutes | Cooking Time: 15 minutes | Serves: 4

Ingredients:
- 2 pears, cored and cut into wedges
- 8 slices of prosciutto
- 1/4 cup blue cheese, crumbled
- Balsamic glaze for drizzling

Instructions:
1. Preheat your Traeger grill to 350°F.
2. Wrap each pear wedge with a slice of prosciutto.
3. Grill the wrapped pears for about 7-8 minutes per side or until the prosciutto is crispy.
4. Arrange the grilled pears on a platter, sprinkle with crumbled blue cheese, and drizzle with balsamic glaze before serving.

Smoked Salmon and Cucumber Bites

Prep Time: 15 minutes | Cooking Time: 0 minutes | Serves: 6

Ingredients:
- 1 cucumber, sliced into rounds
- Smoked salmon slices
- Cream cheese
- Fresh dill, for garnish

Instructions:

1. Spread cream cheese on each cucumber round.
2. Top with a piece of smoked salmon.
3. Garnish with fresh dill before serving.

Grilled Stuffed Mushrooms

Prep Time: 20 minutes | Cooking Time: 15 minutes | Serves: 4

Ingredients:
- 12 large mushrooms, stems removed
- 1/2 cup Italian sausage, cooked and crumbled
- 1/4 cup breadcrumbs
- 1/4 cup grated Parmesan cheese
- 2 tablespoons chopped parsley
- Salt and pepper to taste
- Olive oil

Instructions:
1. Preheat your Traeger grill to 375°F.
2. In a bowl, mix Italian sausage, breadcrumbs, Parmesan cheese, parsley, salt, and pepper.
3. Stuff each mushroom cap with the sausage mixture.
4. Drizzle olive oil over the stuffed mushrooms.
5. Grill for about 15 minutes until mushrooms are tender and filling is golden.

Halloumi Cheese Skewers

Prep Time: 10 minutes | Cooking Time: 5 minutes | Serves: 4

Ingredients:
- 1 block Halloumi cheese, cut into cubes
- Cherry tomatoes
- Red onion, cut into chunks
- Olive oil
- Lemon wedges for serving

Instructions:
1. Preheat your Traeger grill to medium-high heat.
2. Thread Halloumi cubes, cherry tomatoes, and red onion onto skewers, alternating.
3. Brush skewers with olive oil.
4. Grill for about 2-3 minutes per side until cheese is golden and vegetables are charred.
5. Serve with lemon wedges for squeezing over the skewers.

Prosciutto-Wrapped Dates

Prep Time: 10 minutes | Cooking Time: 10 minutes | Serves: 4

Ingredients:
- 12 Medjool dates, pitted
- 6 slices prosciutto, cut in half lengthwise
- Goat cheese (optional)
- Balsamic glaze for drizzling

Instructions:
1. Preheat your Traeger grill to medium heat.
2. If using, stuff each date with a small amount of goat cheese.
3. Wrap each date with a half slice of prosciutto.
4. Secure with a toothpick if needed.
5. Grill the wrapped dates for about 5 minutes per side until prosciutto is crispy.
6. Drizzle with balsamic glaze before serving.

Bacon-Wrapped Asparagus Bundles

Prep Time: 10 minutes | Cooking Time: 10 minutes | Serves: 4

Ingredients:
- 1 pound asparagus spears, tough ends trimmed
- 8 slices bacon
- Olive oil
- Salt and pepper to taste
- Lemon wedges for serving

Instructions:
1. Preheat your Traeger grill to 400°F.
2. Toss asparagus spears with olive oil, salt, and pepper.
3. Bundle 4-5 asparagus spears together and wrap with a slice of bacon.
4. Secure the bacon with toothpicks if needed.
5. Grill the bundles for about 5 minutes per side, or until the bacon is crispy and asparagus is tender.
6. Serve with lemon wedges for squeezing over the bundles.

Zucchini Rolls with Herbed Cream Cheese

Prep Time: 15 minutes | Cooking Time: 10 minutes | Serves: 4

Ingredients:
- 2 large zucchinis, thinly sliced lengthwise
- Olive oil
- Salt and pepper to taste
- 1/2 cup cream cheese, softened
- 2 tablespoons chopped fresh herbs (such as basil, parsley, or chives)
- Lemon zest

Instructions:
1. Preheat your Traeger grill to medium-high heat.
2. Brush zucchini slices with olive oil and season with salt and pepper.
3. Grill the zucchini slices for about 2-3 minutes per side until tender and grill marks appear.
4. In a bowl, mix softened cream cheese with chopped herbs and lemon zest.
5. Spread a thin layer of herbed cream cheese on each grilled zucchini slice.
6. Roll up the zucchini slices and secure with toothpicks.
7. Serve chilled or at room temperature.

Smoked Paprika and Garlic Grilled Shrimp

Prep Time: 15 minutes | Cooking Time: 5 minutes | Serves: 4

Ingredients:
- 1 pound large shrimp, peeled and deveined
- 2 tablespoons olive oil
- 2 cloves garlic, minced
- 1 teaspoon smoked paprika
- Salt and pepper to taste
- Lemon wedges for serving

Instructions:
1. Preheat your Traeger grill to high heat.
2. In a bowl, mix olive oil, minced garlic, smoked paprika, salt, and pepper.
3. Toss the shrimp in the marinade until evenly coated.
4. Thread the shrimp onto skewers.
5. Grill the shrimp skewers for about 2-3 minutes per side until opaque and cooked through.
6. Serve with lemon wedges for squeezing over the shrimp.

Grilled Stuffed Mini Peppers

Prep Time: 20 minutes | **Cooking Time:** 10 minutes | **Serves:** 4

Ingredients:
- 12 mini bell peppers, halved and seeded
- 1 cup cooked quinoa
- 1/2 cup black beans, rinsed and drained
- 1/2 cup corn kernels
- 1/4 cup chopped fresh cilantro
- 1 teaspoon ground cumin
- Salt and pepper to taste
- Shredded cheese (optional)
- Sour cream and salsa for serving

Instructions:
1. Preheat your Traeger grill to 375°F.
2. In a bowl, mix cooked quinoa, black beans, corn, cilantro, cumin, salt, and pepper.
3. Stuff each mini pepper half with the quinoa mixture.
4. If desired, sprinkle shredded cheese on top of the stuffed peppers.
5. Grill the stuffed peppers for about 8-10 minutes until peppers are tender and filling is heated through.
6. Serve with sour cream and salsa on the side.

Grilled Chicken Satay Skewers with Peanut Sauce

Prep Time: 20 minutes | **Cooking Time:** 10 minutes | **Serves:** 4

Ingredients:
- 1 pound boneless, skinless chicken breasts, cut into strips
- Wooden skewers, soaked in water for 30 minutes
- 1/4 cup soy sauce
- 2 tablespoons honey
- 2 cloves garlic, minced
- 1 teaspoon ground cumin
- 1/2 teaspoon ground coriander
- Peanut sauce for dipping

Instructions:
1. Preheat your Traeger grill to medium-high heat.
2. Thread chicken strips onto soaked skewers.
3. In a bowl, whisk together soy sauce, honey, minced garlic, cumin, and coriander.
4. Brush the chicken skewers with the marinade.

5. Grill the chicken skewers for about 4-5 minutes per side until cooked through and slightly charred.
6. Serve the chicken satay skewers with peanut sauce for dipping.

Grilled Stuffed Portobello Mushrooms

Prep Time: 15 minutes | **Cooking Time:** 15 minutes | **Serves:** 4

Ingredients:
- 4 large portobello mushrooms, stems removed
- 1 cup spinach, chopped
- 1/2 cup sun-dried tomatoes, chopped
- 1/2 cup feta cheese, crumbled
- 2 tablespoons olive oil
- Salt and pepper to taste

Instructions:
1. Preheat your Traeger grill to 375°F.
2. In a bowl, mix together chopped spinach, sun-dried tomatoes, feta cheese, olive oil, salt, and pepper.
3. Stuff each portobello mushroom with the spinach mixture.
4. Grill the stuffed mushrooms for about 10-15 minutes until the mushrooms are tender and the filling is heated through.
5. Serve hot as an appetizer or a light snack.

Smoked Chicken Wings with Honey Sriracha Glaze

Prep Time: 10 minutes | **Cooking Time:** 45 minutes | **Serves:** 4

Ingredients:
- 2 pounds chicken wings
- 1/4 cup soy sauce
- 2 tablespoons honey
- 2 tablespoons Sriracha sauce
- 2 cloves garlic, minced
- Salt and pepper to taste
- Sesame seeds and chopped green onions for garnish

Instructions:
1. Preheat your Traeger grill to 375°F.
2. In a bowl, whisk together soy sauce, honey, Sriracha sauce, minced garlic, salt, and pepper.
3. Toss the chicken wings in the marinade until evenly coated.
4. Arrange the wings on the grill grates and smoke for

about 30 minutes.

5. Increase the temperature to 400°F and grill for an additional 10-15 minutes, turning occasionally, until the wings are cooked through and crispy.

6. Garnish with sesame seeds and chopped green onions before serving.

Grilled Caprese Skewers

Prep Time: 15 minutes | Cooking Time: 5 minutes | Serves: 4

Ingredients:
- Cherry tomatoes
- Fresh mozzarella balls
- Fresh basil leaves
- Balsamic glaze for drizzling
- Wooden skewers

Instructions:
1. Preheat your Traeger grill to medium-high heat.
2. Thread cherry tomatoes, fresh mozzarella balls, and fresh basil leaves onto skewers, alternating.
3. Grill the skewers for about 2-3 minutes per side until the cheese starts to melt and tomatoes are slightly charred.
4. Drizzle with balsamic glaze before serving.

Grilled Flatbread with Pesto and Sun-Dried Tomatoes

Prep Time: 10 minutes | Cooking Time: 10 minutes | Serves: 4

Ingredients:
- 2 store-bought flatbreads
- 1/2 cup pesto sauce
- 1/4 cup sun-dried tomatoes, chopped
- 1/4 cup shredded mozzarella cheese
- Fresh basil leaves for garnish

Instructions:
1. Preheat your Traeger grill to 400°F.
2. Spread pesto sauce evenly over each flatbread.
3. Sprinkle chopped sun-dried tomatoes and shredded mozzarella cheese on top.
4. Place the flatbreads directly on the grill grates and cook for about 5 minutes per side, or until the cheese is melted and the edges are crispy.
5. Remove from the grill, garnish with fresh basil leaves, and slice into wedges before serving.

Grilled Corn and Avocado Salad Cups

Prep Time: 15 minutes | Cooking Time: 10 minutes | Serves: 4

Ingredients:
- 2 ears of corn, husked
- 1 avocado, diced
- 1/2 cup cherry tomatoes, halved
- 1/4 cup red onion, finely chopped
- 2 tablespoons fresh cilantro, chopped
- Juice of 1 lime
- Salt and pepper to taste
- Tortilla cups or small lettuce leaves for serving

Instructions:
1. Preheat your Traeger grill to 400°F.
2. Grill the corn for about 8-10 minutes, turning occasionally, until charred and tender.
3. Cut the kernels off the cob and place them in a bowl.
4. Add diced avocado, cherry tomatoes, red onion, chopped cilantro, lime juice, salt, and pepper to the bowl.
5. Mix well to combine all ingredients.
6. Serve the corn and avocado salad in tortilla cups or on small lettuce leaves as individual appetizer cups.

Grilled Teriyaki Pineapple Chicken Skewers

Prep Time: 30 minutes | Cooking Time: 10 minutes | Serves: 4

Ingredients:
- 1 pound chicken breast, cut into cubes
- 1 cup pineapple chunks
- 1/2 cup teriyaki sauce
- Wooden skewers, soaked in water
- Sesame seeds for garnish
- Chopped green onions for garnish

Instructions:
1. In a bowl, marinate chicken cubes in teriyaki sauce for at least 20 minutes.
2. Preheat your Traeger grill to medium heat.
3. Thread marinated chicken cubes and pineapple chunks onto skewers, alternating.
4. Grill the skewers for about 4-5 minutes per side until chicken is cooked through and pineapple is caramelized.

5. Garnish with sesame seeds and chopped green onions before serving.

Grilled Stuffed Mini Bell Peppers and Bacon

Prep Time: 15 minutes | Cooking Time: 10 minutes | Serves: 4

Ingredients:
- 12 mini bell peppers, halved and seeded
- 1/2 cup cream cheese, softened
- 6 slices bacon, cooked and crumbled
- 2 tablespoons chopped chives
- Salt and pepper to taste

Instructions:
1. Preheat your Traeger grill to 375°F.
2. In a bowl, mix softened cream cheese, cooked bacon crumbles, chopped chives, salt, and pepper.
3. Stuff each mini bell pepper half with the cream cheese mixture.
4. Grill the stuffed peppers for about 8-10 minutes until peppers are tender and filling is heated through.
5. Serve hot as a delightful appetizer.

Grilled Pita Bread with Herbed Yogurt Dip

Prep Time: 10 minutes | Cooking Time: 5 minutes | Serves: 4

Ingredients:
- 4 whole wheat pita bread rounds
- Olive oil
- Salt and pepper to taste
- 1 cup Greek yogurt
- 2 tablespoons chopped fresh herbs (such as dill, parsley, and mint)
- 1 clove garlic, minced
- Lemon juice to taste

Instructions:
1. Preheat your Traeger grill to medium-high heat.
2. Brush pita bread rounds with olive oil and season with salt and pepper.
3. Grill the pita bread for about 1-2 minutes per side until lightly charred and crispy.
4. In a bowl, mix Greek yogurt, chopped fresh herbs, minced garlic, and lemon juice.
5. Serve grilled pita bread with herbed yogurt dip on the side.

Grilled Cajun Shrimp Lettuce Wraps

Prep Time: 20 minutes | Cooking Time: 5 minutes | Serves: 4

Ingredients:
- 1 pound large shrimp, peeled and deveined
- Cajun seasoning to taste
- Olive oil
- Bibb lettuce leaves
- Sliced avocado
- Sliced red onion
- Sliced bell peppers
- Lime wedges for serving

Instructions:
1. Preheat your Traeger grill to medium-high heat.
2. Season shrimp with Cajun seasoning and drizzle with olive oil.
3. Grill the shrimp for about 2-3 minutes per side until pink and cooked through.
4. Arrange Bibb lettuce leaves on a serving platter.
5. Fill lettuce leaves with grilled Cajun shrimp, sliced avocado, red onion, and bell peppers.
6. Squeeze lime juice over the wraps before serving.

Grilled Artichoke Hearts with Lemon Aioli

Prep Time: 15 minutes | Cooking Time: 10 minutes | Serves: 4

Ingredients:
- 1 can (14 oz) artichoke hearts, drained and halved
- Olive oil
- Salt and pepper to taste
- Lemon wedges for serving

Lemon Aioli:
- 1/2 cup mayonnaise
- 1 clove garlic, minced
- 1 tablespoon fresh lemon juice
- Zest of 1 lemon
- Salt and pepper to taste

Instructions:
1. Preheat your Traeger grill to medium-high heat.
2. Brush artichoke hearts with olive oil and season with salt and pepper.
3. Grill the artichoke hearts for about 4-5 minutes per side until lightly charred.

4. In a bowl, mix together mayonnaise, minced garlic, lemon juice, lemon zest, salt, and pepper to make the aioli.

5. Serve grilled artichoke hearts with lemon aioli and lemon wedges on the side.

Grilled Vegetable Quesadillas

Prep Time: 20 minutes | Cooking Time: 10 minutes | Serves: 4

Ingredients:
- 4 large flour tortillas
- 1 zucchini, sliced
- 1 yellow squash, sliced
- 1 red bell pepper, sliced
- 1 red onion, sliced
- Olive oil
- Salt and pepper to taste
- Shredded cheese
- Guacamole and sour cream for serving

Instructions:
1. Preheat your Traeger grill to medium heat.
2. Toss zucchini, yellow squash, red bell pepper, and red onion slices with olive oil, salt, and pepper.
3. Grill the vegetables for about 3-4 minutes per side until tender and lightly charred.
4. Lay out a tortilla and sprinkle shredded cheese on one half.
5. Arrange grilled vegetables over the cheese and fold the tortilla in half.
6. Grill the quesadilla for about 2-3 minutes per side until cheese is melted and tortilla is crispy.
7. Slice into wedges and serve with guacamole and sour cream.

Stuffed Jalapeños with Cream Cheese and Bacon

Prep Time: 20 minutes | Cooking Time: 10 minutes | Serves: 4

Ingredients:
- 8 large jalapeño peppers, halved and seeded
- 1/2 cup cream cheese, softened
- 4 slices bacon, cooked and crumbled
- 2 tablespoons chopped fresh cilantro
- 1 teaspoon garlic powder
- Salt and pepper to taste

Instructions:
1. Preheat your Traeger grill to 375°F.
2. In a bowl, mix softened cream cheese, cooked bacon crumbles, chopped cilantro, garlic powder, salt, and pepper.
3. Stuff each jalapeño half with the cream cheese mixture.
4. Grill the stuffed jalapeños for about 8-10 minutes until peppers are tender and filling is bubbly.
5. Serve hot as a spicy and savory snack.

Sweet Potato Fries with Chipotle Dip

Prep Time: 15 minutes | Cooking Time: 20 minutes | Serves: 4

Ingredients:
- 2 large sweet potatoes, peeled and cut into fries
- Olive oil
- Salt and pepper to taste
- 1/2 cup mayonnaise
- 1-2 chipotle peppers in adobo sauce, minced
- 1 tablespoon adobo sauce
- Juice of 1 lime
- Chopped fresh cilantro for garnish

Instructions:
1. Preheat your Traeger grill to 400°F.
2. Toss sweet potato fries with olive oil, salt, and pepper.
3. Grill the sweet potato fries for about 15-20 minutes, turning occasionally, until crispy and golden.
4. In a bowl, mix together mayonnaise, minced chipotle peppers, adobo sauce, and lime juice to make the dip.
5. Sprinkle chopped cilantro over the grilled sweet potato fries and serve with chipotle dip.

Prosciutto-Wrapped Asparagus

Prep Time: 10 minutes | Cooking Time: 8 minutes | Serves: 4

Ingredients:
- 1 pound asparagus spears, trimmed
- Olive oil
- Salt and pepper to taste
- 8 slices prosciutto
- Lemon wedges for serving

Instructions:
1. Preheat your Traeger grill to medium-high heat.
2. Toss asparagus spears with olive oil, salt, and pepper.
3. Wrap each asparagus spear with a slice of prosciutto.
4. Grill the prosciutto-wrapped asparagus for about 3-4 minutes per side until asparagus is tender and prosciutto is crispy.
5. Squeeze lemon juice over the grilled asparagus before serving.

Eggplant Caprese Salad
Prep Time: 15 minutes | Cooking Time: 10 minutes | Serves: 4

Ingredients:
- 1 large eggplant, sliced into rounds
- Olive oil
- Salt and pepper to taste
- Cherry tomatoes, halved
- Fresh mozzarella cheese, sliced
- Fresh basil leaves
- Balsamic glaze for drizzling

Instructions:
1. Preheat your Traeger grill to medium heat.
2. Brush eggplant slices with olive oil and season with salt and pepper.
3. Grill the eggplant slices for about 3-4 minutes per side until tender and grill marks appear.
4. Assemble the grilled eggplant, cherry tomatoes, mozzarella slices, and fresh basil leaves on a platter.
5. Drizzle with balsamic glaze before serving.

Honey Sriracha Chicken Wings
Prep Time: 10 minutes | Cooking Time: 25 minutes | Serves: 4

Ingredients:
- 2 pounds chicken wings
- Olive oil
- Salt and pepper to taste
- 1/4 cup honey
- 2 tablespoons Sriracha sauce
- 2 tablespoons soy sauce
- Sesame seeds and chopped green onions for garnish

Instructions:
1. Preheat your Traeger grill to 375°F.
2. Toss chicken wings with olive oil, salt, and pepper.
3. Grill the chicken wings for about 20-25 minutes, turning occasionally, until cooked through and crispy.
4. In a bowl, mix honey, Sriracha sauce, and soy sauce to make the glaze.
5. Brush the grilled chicken wings with the honey Sriracha glaze.
6. Grill for an additional 2-3 minutes to caramelize the glaze.
7. Garnish with sesame seeds and chopped green onions before serving.

Stuffed Mini Potatoes with Bacon and Cheese
Prep Time: 20 minutes | Cooking Time: 25 minutes | Serves: 4

Ingredients:
- 12 baby potatoes
- Olive oil
- Salt and pepper to taste
- 4 slices bacon, cooked and crumbled
- 1/2 cup shredded cheddar cheese
- Sour cream and chopped chives for garnish

Instructions:
1. Preheat your Traeger grill to 400°F.
2. Toss baby potatoes with olive oil, salt, and pepper.
3. Grill the potatoes for about 20-25 minutes until tender, turning occasionally.
4. Remove potatoes from the grill and let cool slightly.
5. Slice off the top of each potato and scoop out some flesh to create a hollow space.
6. Fill each potato with crumbled bacon and shredded cheddar cheese.
7. Return stuffed potatoes to the grill for 5 minutes or until cheese is melted and bubbly.
8. Garnish with sour cream and chopped chives before serving.

Prosciutto-Wrapped Pears with Goat Cheese
Prep Time: 15 minutes | Cooking Time: 10 minutes | Serves: 4

Ingredients:
- 2 ripe pears, halved and cored
- Olive oil
- Salt and pepper to taste
- 4 slices prosciutto

- 1/4 cup crumbled goat cheese
- Honey for drizzling

Instructions:
1. Preheat your Traeger grill to medium-high heat.
2. Brush pear halves with olive oil and season with salt and pepper.
3. Wrap each pear half with a slice of prosciutto.
4. Grill the prosciutto-wrapped pears for about 4-5 minutes per side until pears are tender and prosciutto is crispy.
5. Remove from the grill and top each pear half with crumbled goat cheese.
6. Drizzle with honey before serving.

Grilled Avocado Stuffed with Quinoa Salad

Prep Time: 20 minutes | Cooking Time: 10 minutes | Serves: 4

Ingredients:
- 2 ripe avocados, halved and pitted
- Olive oil
- Salt and pepper to taste
- 1 cup cooked quinoa
- 1/2 cup cherry tomatoes, halved
- 1/4 cup diced cucumber
- 1/4 cup chopped red onion
- 2 tablespoons chopped fresh cilantro
- Juice of 1 lime

Instructions:
1. Preheat your Traeger grill to medium heat.
2. Brush avocado halves with olive oil and season with salt and pepper.
3. Grill the avocado halves for about 2-3 minutes per side until grill marks appear.
4. In a bowl, mix cooked quinoa, cherry tomatoes, cucumber, red onion, cilantro, lime juice, salt, and pepper to make the salad.
5. Spoon quinoa salad into the grilled avocado halves.
6. Top with crumbled feta cheese if desired before serving.

Grilled Stuffed Mushrooms with Herb Cheese

Prep Time: 15 minutes | Cooking Time: 15 minutes | Serves: 4

Ingredients:
- 12 large mushroom caps
- 1/2 cup herb cheese spread (such as Boursin)
- 2 tablespoons grated Parmesan cheese
- 2 tablespoons chopped fresh parsley
- Salt and pepper to taste
- Olive oil

Instructions:
1. Preheat your Traeger grill to 375°F.
2. Remove the stems from the mushroom caps and brush the caps with olive oil.
3. In a bowl, mix herb cheese spread, grated Parmesan, chopped parsley, salt, and pepper.
4. Stuff each mushroom cap with the cheese mixture.
5. Place stuffed mushrooms on the grill and cook for about 10-15 minutes until the cheese is melted and bubbly.

Grilled Shrimp and Pineapple Skewers

Prep Time: 20 minutes | Cooking Time: 10 minutes | Serves: 4

Ingredients:
- 1 pound large shrimp, peeled and deveined
- 1 cup pineapple chunks
- Wooden skewers, soaked in water
- 1/2 cup coconut milk
- Zest and juice of 1 lime
- 2 tablespoons honey
- Salt and pepper to taste
- Chopped cilantro for garnish

Instructions:
1. In a bowl, whisk together coconut milk, lime zest, lime juice, honey, salt, and pepper to make the marinade.
2. Add shrimp and pineapple chunks to the marinade, cover, and refrigerate for at least 30 minutes.
3. Preheat your Traeger grill to medium-high heat.
4. Thread marinated shrimp and pineapple onto skewers, alternating.
5. Grill the skewers for about 3-4 minutes per side until shrimp are pink and cooked through.
6. Garnish with chopped cilantro before serving.

Stuffed Mini Bell Peppers with Creamy Spinach

Prep Time: 20 minutes | Cooking Time: 15 minutes | Serves: 4

Ingredients:
- 12 mini bell peppers, halved and seeded
- 1 cup creamy spinach and artichoke dip
- Shredded mozzarella cheese
- Chopped fresh parsley for garnish

Instructions:
1. Preheat your Traeger grill to 375°F.
2. Fill each mini bell pepper half with creamy spinach and artichoke dip.
3. Sprinkle shredded mozzarella cheese over the stuffed peppers.
4. Place stuffed peppers on the grill and cook for about 10-15 minutes until peppers are tender and filling is heated through.
5. Garnish with chopped parsley before serving.

Grilled Watermelon and Feta Skewers

Prep Time: 15 minutes | Cooking Time: 5 minutes | Serves: 4

Ingredients:
- 1/2 small seedless watermelon, cut into cubes
- Feta cheese, cut into cubes
- Wooden skewers, soaked in water
- Balsamic glaze

Instructions:
1. Preheat your Traeger grill to medium-high heat.
2. Thread watermelon cubes and feta cheese cubes onto skewers, alternating.
3. Grill the skewers for about 1-2 minutes per side until grill marks appear.
4. Arrange grilled skewers on a serving platter.
5. Drizzle with balsamic glaze before serving.

Grilled Corn and Black Bean Salsa

Prep Time: 20 minutes | Cooking Time: 10 minutes | Serves: 4

Ingredients:
- 2 ears of corn, husked
- 1 can (15 oz) black beans, rinsed and drained
- 1/2 red onion, finely chopped
- 1 jalapeño pepper, seeded and finely chopped
- 1/4 cup chopped fresh cilantro
- Juice of 2 limes
- Salt and pepper to taste
- Tortilla chips (store-bought or homemade)

Instructions:
1. Preheat your Traeger grill to medium heat.
2. Grill the corn for about 8-10 minutes, turning occasionally, until kernels are lightly charred.
3. Cut the kernels off the cob and place them in a bowl.
4. Add black beans, chopped red onion, jalapeño pepper, cilantro, lime juice, salt, and pepper to the bowl.
5. Mix well to combine all ingredients.
6. Serve the grilled corn and black bean salsa with tortilla chips.

Grilled Prosciutto–Wrapped Dates with Goat Cheese

Prep Time: 15 minutes | Cooking Time: 5 minutes | Serves: 4

Ingredients:
- 12 Medjool dates, pitted
- 4 ounces goat cheese
- 6 slices prosciutto, cut in half lengthwise
- Balsamic glaze for drizzling
- Toothpicks

Instructions:
1. Preheat your Traeger grill to medium-high heat.
2. Stuff each date with a small amount of goat cheese.
3. Wrap each stuffed date with a half slice of prosciutto and secure with a toothpick.
4. Grill the prosciutto-wrapped dates for about 2-3 minutes per side until the prosciutto is crispy and lightly charred.
5. Drizzle with balsamic glaze before serving.

Grilled Bruschetta with Tomato and Basil

Prep Time: 15 minutes | Cooking Time: 5 minutes | Serves: 4

Ingredients:
- 1 baguette, sliced into rounds
- Olive oil
- 2 cups cherry tomatoes, halved

- 1/4 cup fresh basil leaves, chopped
- 2 cloves garlic, minced
- Balsamic glaze for drizzling
- Salt and pepper to taste

Instructions:
1. Preheat your Traeger grill to medium-high heat.
2. Brush baguette slices with olive oil and grill for about 1-2 minutes per side until lightly toasted.
3. In a bowl, mix cherry tomatoes, chopped basil, minced garlic, salt, and pepper.
4. Spoon the tomato mixture onto grilled baguette slices.
5. Drizzle with balsamic glaze before serving.

Grilled Avocado Toast with Smoked Salmon
Prep Time: 10 minutes | Cooking Time: 5 minutes | Serves: 4

Ingredients:
- 2 ripe avocados, mashed
- 4 slices whole grain bread
- Olive oil
- Salt and pepper to taste
- Smoked salmon slices
- Fresh dill for garnish
- Lemon wedges for serving

Instructions:
1. Preheat your Traeger grill to medium heat.
2. Brush whole grain bread slices with olive oil and grill for about 1-2 minutes per side until toasted.
3. Spread mashed avocado on grilled bread slices.
4. Top with smoked salmon slices.
5. Garnish with fresh dill and serve with lemon wedges.

Grilled Halloumi Cheese Skewers
Prep Time: 15 minutes | Cooking Time: 5 minutes | Serves: 4

Ingredients:
- 1 block Halloumi cheese, cut into cubes
- Olive oil
- Wooden skewers, soaked in water
- Fresh parsley, chopped
- Fresh cilantro, chopped
- 2 cloves garlic, minced
- Red pepper flakes (optional)

- Lemon juice
- Salt and pepper to taste

Instructions:
1. Preheat your Traeger grill to medium-high heat.
2. Thread Halloumi cheese cubes onto skewers.
3. Brush cheese skewers with olive oil and season with salt and pepper.
4. Grill the skewers for about 2-3 minutes per side until grill marks appear and cheese is heated through.
5. In a bowl, mix chopped parsley, chopped cilantro, minced garlic, red pepper flakes (if using), lemon juice, salt, and pepper to make the chimichurri sauce.
6. Drizzle the grilled Halloumi skewers with chimichurri sauce before serving.

Grilled Stuffed Baby Bell Peppers
Prep Time: 20 minutes | Cooking Time: 10 minutes | Serves: 4

Ingredients:
- 12 baby bell peppers, halved and seeded
- 1 cup creamy herb cheese (such as Alouette)
- Fresh chives, chopped
- Fresh parsley, chopped
- Salt and pepper to taste

Instructions:
1. Preheat your Traeger grill to 375°F.
2. Fill each baby bell pepper half with creamy herb cheese.
3. Sprinkle chopped chives and parsley over the stuffed peppers.
4. Place stuffed peppers on the grill and cook for about 8-10 minutes until peppers are tender and filling is heated through.
5. Serve hot as a delightful appetizer.

Grilled Zucchini Roll-Ups
Prep Time: 15 minutes | Cooking Time: 10 minutes | Serves: 4

Ingredients:
- 2 medium zucchinis, sliced lengthwise into thin strips
- Olive oil
- Salt and pepper to taste
- 1/2 cup cream cheese, softened
- 2 tablespoons chopped fresh herbs (such as basil,

parsley, and chives)
- Sun-dried tomatoes, chopped (optional)
- Toothpicks

Instructions:
1. Preheat your Traeger grill to medium-high heat.
2. Brush zucchini strips with olive oil and season with salt and pepper.
3. Grill the zucchini strips for about 1-2 minutes per side until tender and lightly charred.
4. In a bowl, mix softened cream cheese with chopped fresh herbs and sun-dried tomatoes (if using).
5. Spread a thin layer of the herbed cream cheese mixture onto each grilled zucchini strip.
6. Roll up the zucchini strips and secure with toothpicks.
7. Grill the zucchini roll-ups for an additional 2-3 minutes to warm the filling.
8. Serve warm as a delicious appetizer.

Grilled Sweet Potato Nachos
Prep Time: 20 minutes | Cooking Time: 15 minutes | Serves: 4

Ingredients:
- 2 large sweet potatoes, thinly sliced into rounds
- Olive oil
- Salt and pepper to taste
- 1 can (15 oz) black beans, rinsed and drained
- Shredded cheddar cheese
- Guacamole, salsa, and sour cream for topping

Instructions:
1. Preheat your Traeger grill to 400°F.
2. Toss sweet potato slices with olive oil, salt, and pepper.
3. Grill the sweet potato slices for about 5-7 minutes per side until tender and lightly charred.
4. Arrange grilled sweet potato slices on a serving platter.
5. Top with black beans and shredded cheddar cheese.
6. Place the nachos back on the grill for a few minutes to melt the cheese.
7. Serve hot with guacamole, salsa, and sour cream on top.

Grilled Halloumi and Veggie Skewers
Prep Time: 20 minutes | Cooking Time: 10 minutes | Serves: 4

Ingredients:
- 1 block Halloumi cheese, cut into cubes
- Cherry tomatoes
- Red onion, cut into chunks
- Bell peppers, cut into chunks
- Zucchini, sliced
- Olive oil
- Salt and pepper to taste
- Wooden skewers, soaked in water

Lemon garlic sauce:
- 1/4 cup olive oil
- Juice of 1 lemon
- 2 cloves garlic, minced
- 1 teaspoon honey
- Salt and pepper to taste
- Chopped fresh parsley for garnish

Instructions:
1. Preheat your Traeger grill to medium-high heat.
2. Thread Halloumi cubes, cherry tomatoes, red onion chunks, bell pepper chunks, and zucchini slices onto skewers, alternating.
3. Brush skewers with olive oil and season with salt and pepper.
4. Grill the skewers for about 3-4 minutes per side until vegetables are tender and Halloumi is golden.
5. In a bowl, whisk together olive oil, lemon juice, minced garlic, honey, salt, and pepper to make the lemon garlic sauce.
6. Drizzle the grilled skewers with lemon garlic sauce and garnish with chopped parsley before serving.

Grilled Stuffed Jalapeños with Cream Cheese

Prep Time: 20 minutes | Cooking Time: 10 minutes | Serves: 4

Ingredients:
- 8 large jalapeño peppers, halved and seeded
- 1/2 cup cream cheese, softened
- 1/2 cup mango salsa (store-bought or homemade)
- Fresh cilantro leaves for garnish

Instructions:
1. Preheat your Traeger grill to 375°F.
2. In a bowl, mix softened cream cheese with mango salsa.
3. Fill each jalapeño half with the cream cheese and mango salsa mixture.
4. Grill the stuffed jalapeños for about 8-10 minutes until peppers are tender and filling is bubbly.
5. Garnish with fresh cilantro leaves before serving.

Grilled Chicken and Pineapple Skewers

Prep Time: 30 minutes | Cooking Time: 10 minutes | Serves: 4

Ingredients:
- 1 pound chicken breast, cut into cubes
- 1 cup pineapple chunks
- Wooden skewers, soaked in water

Teriyaki glaze:
- 1/4 cup soy sauce
- 2 tablespoons honey
- 1 tablespoon rice vinegar
- 1 clove garlic, minced
- 1 teaspoon grated ginger
- 1 tablespoon cornstarch mixed with 2 tablespoons water
- Sesame seeds for garnish

Instructions:
1. In a bowl, whisk together soy sauce, honey, rice vinegar, minced garlic, grated ginger, and cornstarch slurry to make the teriyaki glaze.
2. Marinate chicken cubes in half of the teriyaki glaze for at least 20 minutes.
3. Preheat your Traeger grill to medium-high heat.
4. Thread marinated chicken cubes and pineapple chunks onto skewers, alternating.
5. Grill the skewers for about 4-5 minutes per side until chicken is cooked through and pineapple is caramelized.
6. Brush remaining teriyaki glaze over the skewers during grilling.
7. Garnish with sesame seeds before serving.

Smoked Turkey Breast

Prep Time: 15 minutes | Cooking Time: 2-3 hours | Serves: 6-8

Ingredients:
- 1 whole turkey breast (bone-in or boneless)
- Olive oil
- Salt and pepper to taste
- Traeger poultry rub or your favorite seasoning blend

Instructions:
1. Preheat your Traeger grill to 225°F using applewood pellets.
2. Rub the turkey breast with olive oil and season generously with salt, pepper, and Traeger poultry rub.
3. Place the turkey breast directly on the grill grate and smoke for 2-3 hours, or until the internal temperature reaches 165°F.
4. Remove from the grill, tent with foil, and let rest for 15-20 minutes before slicing.
5. Serve the smoked turkey breast with your favorite sides and sauces.

BBQ Chicken Wings

Prep Time: 10 minutes | Cooking Time: 45-60 minutes | Serves: 4-6

Ingredients:
- 2 pounds chicken wings
- Olive oil
- Salt and pepper to taste
- Traeger chicken rub or your favorite BBQ seasoning
- Your choice of BBQ sauce

Instructions:
1. Preheat your Traeger grill to 375°F.
2. Toss chicken wings with olive oil, salt, pepper, and Traeger chicken rub.
3. Arrange the wings on the grill grate and cook for 45-60 minutes, turning occasionally, until golden and crispy.
4. Brush the wings with BBQ sauce during the last 10 minutes of cooking for extra flavor.
5. Remove from the grill and serve hot with additional BBQ sauce for dipping.

Grilled Chicken Caesar Salad

Prep Time: 20 minutes | Cooking Time: 15 minutes | Serves: 4

Ingredients:
- 2 boneless, skinless chicken breasts
- Olive oil
- Salt and pepper to taste
- Romaine lettuce, chopped
- Croutons
- Shaved Parmesan cheese
- Caesar dressing

Instructions:
1. Preheat your Traeger grill to medium-high heat.
2. Brush chicken breasts with olive oil and season with salt and pepper.
3. Grill the chicken breasts for about 6-8 minutes per side until cooked through and grill marks appear.
4. Remove from the grill and let rest for a few minutes before slicing.
5. In a large bowl, toss chopped romaine lettuce with Caesar dressing.
6. Arrange grilled chicken slices, croutons, and shaved Parmesan cheese on top of the salad.
7. Serve the Traeger grilled chicken Caesar salad as a delicious and satisfying meal.

Maple Glazed Duck Breast

Prep Time: 10 minutes | Cooking Time: 15-20 minutes | Serves: 2-4

Ingredients:
- 2 duck breasts
- Salt and pepper to taste
- Maple syrup
- Dijon mustard
- Fresh thyme leaves

Instructions:
1. Preheat your Traeger grill to 375°F.
2. Score the skin of the duck breasts in a criss-cross pattern and season with salt and pepper.
3. In a bowl, mix together maple syrup, Dijon mustard, and fresh thyme leaves.
4. Brush the duck breasts with the maple glaze mixture.
5. Place the duck breasts directly on the grill grate, skin-side down, and cook for 10-12 minutes.
6. Flip the duck breasts, brush with more maple glaze,

and continue cooking for another 5-8 minutes or until desired doneness (medium-rare to medium).
7. Remove from the grill, let rest for a few minutes, then slice and serve with extra maple glaze.

Smoked Cornish Hens

Prep Time: 15 minutes | Cooking Time: 2-3 hours | Serves: 2-4

Ingredients:
- 2 Cornish hens
- Olive oil
- Salt and pepper to taste
- Traeger poultry rub or your favorite seasoning blend

Instructions:
1. Preheat your Traeger grill to 225°F using applewood pellets.
2. Rub Cornish hens with olive oil and season inside and out with salt, pepper, and Traeger poultry rub.
3. Tie the legs together with kitchen twine for even cooking.
4. Place the Cornish hens directly on the grill grate and smoke for 2-3 hours, or until the internal temperature reaches 165°F in the thickest part of the thigh.
5. Remove from the grill, tent with foil, and let rest for 10-15 minutes before serving.
6. Serve the Traeger smoked Cornish hens with your favorite sides for a delightful meal.

Smoked Chicken Thighs with Lemon Herb Butter

Prep Time: 15 minutes | Cooking Time: 1 hour | Serves: 4

Ingredients:
- 4 chicken thighs, bone-in and skin-on
- Olive oil
- Salt and pepper to taste
- Traeger chicken rub or your favorite seasoning blend

Lemon herb butter:
- 4 tablespoons unsalted butter, softened
- Zest of 1 lemon
- 2 tablespoons chopped fresh herbs (such as thyme, rosemary, and parsley)
- Salt and pepper to taste

Instructions:

1. Preheat your Traeger grill to 375°F.
2. Rub chicken thighs with olive oil and season with salt, pepper, and Traeger chicken rub.
3. In a bowl, mix softened butter, lemon zest, chopped fresh herbs, salt, and pepper to make the lemon herb butter.
4. Gently lift the skin of each chicken thigh and spread some lemon herb butter underneath.
5. Place the chicken thighs directly on the grill grate, skin-side up.
6. Smoke the chicken thighs for about 45-60 minutes or until the internal temperature reaches 165°F.
7. Remove from the grill and let rest for a few minutes before serving.

Turkey Burgers with Avocado Mayo

Prep Time: 20 minutes | Cooking Time: 20 minutes | Serves: 4

Ingredients:
- 1 pound ground turkey
- 1/4 cup breadcrumbs
- 1/4 cup grated Parmesan cheese
- 1 teaspoon garlic powder
- Salt and pepper to taste
- Olive oil
- Burger buns
- Lettuce, tomato slices, and red onion slices for topping

Avocado mayo:
- 1 ripe avocado, mashed
- 1/4 cup mayonnaise
- 1 tablespoon lime juice
- Salt and pepper to taste

Instructions:
1. Preheat your Traeger grill to 375°F.
2. In a bowl, mix ground turkey, breadcrumbs, grated Parmesan, garlic powder, salt, and pepper until well combined.
3. Divide the mixture into 4 equal portions and form into burger patties.
4. Brush burger patties with olive oil and place them on the grill grate.
5. Smoke the turkey burgers for about 18-20 minutes, flipping once halfway through, until cooked through.
6. While the burgers are cooking, prepare the avocado mayo by mixing mashed avocado, mayonnaise, lime

juice, salt, and pepper in a bowl.

7. Toast burger buns on the grill during the last few minutes of cooking.

8. Assemble burgers with lettuce, tomato slices, red onion slices, and a dollop of avocado mayo on top.

9. Serve the Traeger smoked turkey burgers hot.

Honey Garlic Glazed Chicken Drumsticks

Prep Time: 15 minutes | Cooking Time: 40 minutes | Serves: 4

Ingredients:

- 8 chicken drumsticks
- Olive oil
- Salt and pepper to taste

Honey garlic glaze:

- 1/4 cup honey
- 2 tablespoons soy sauce
- 1 tablespoon minced garlic
- 1 teaspoon grated ginger
- Red pepper flakes (optional)
- Sesame seeds for garnish

Instructions:

1. Preheat your Traeger grill to 375°F.

2. Brush chicken drumsticks with olive oil and season with salt and pepper.

3. Place the drumsticks directly on the grill grate.

4. Grill the chicken drumsticks for about 30-35 minutes, turning occasionally, until golden and cooked through.

5. In a small saucepan, combine honey, soy sauce, minced garlic, grated ginger, and red pepper flakes.

6. Heat the honey garlic glaze over medium heat until it thickens slightly.

7. Brush the grilled chicken drumsticks with the honey garlic glaze during the last 5-10 minutes of cooking.

8. Remove from the grill and sprinkle with sesame seeds before serving.

Duck Breast with Orange Glaze

Prep Time: 15 minutes | Cooking Time: 30 minutes | Serves: 2-3

Ingredients:

- 2 duck breasts
- Salt and pepper to taste

Orange glaze:

- 1/2 cup orange juice
- Zest of 1 orange
- 2 tablespoons honey
- 1 tablespoon soy sauce
- 1 teaspoon Dijon mustard
- Salt and pepper to taste

Instructions:

1. Preheat your Traeger grill to 375°F.

2. Score the skin of the duck breasts in a criss-cross pattern and season with salt and pepper.

3. In a saucepan, combine orange juice, orange zest, honey, soy sauce, Dijon mustard, salt, and pepper to make the orange glaze.

4. Simmer the glaze over medium heat until it thickens slightly.

5. Place the duck breasts directly on the grill grate, skin-side down.

6. Smoke the duck breasts for about 15 minutes, then brush with the orange glaze.

7. Continue smoking for another 10-15 minutes or until the internal temperature reaches your desired doneness.

8. Remove from the grill, let rest for a few minutes, then slice and serve with extra orange glaze.

Grilled Chicken Caesar Pizza

Prep Time: 20 minutes | Cooking Time: 15 minutes | Serves: 4

Ingredients:

- 1 pound pizza dough
- Olive oil
- Salt and pepper to taste
- 1 cup cooked chicken breast, shredded
- Caesar dressing
- Shredded mozzarella cheese
- Grated Parmesan cheese
- Chopped romaine lettuce
- Croutons

Instructions:

1. Preheat your Traeger grill to 450°F.

2. Roll out pizza dough on a floured surface to desired thickness.

3. Brush olive oil over the pizza dough and season with salt and pepper.

4. Spread a layer of Caesar dressing over the dough.

5. Top with shredded chicken, mozzarella cheese, and grated Parmesan cheese.
6. Place the pizza directly on the grill grate and cook for about 10-15 minutes or until the crust is golden and cheese is melted and bubbly.
7. Remove from the grill and top with chopped romaine lettuce and croutons before serving.

Smoked Quail with Cherry Glaze
Prep Time: 20 minutes | Cooking Time: 30 minutes | Serves: 4

Ingredients:
• 8 quail, halved and deboned
• Olive oil
• Salt and pepper to taste

Cherry glaze:
• 1 cup cherry preserves
• 2 tablespoons balsamic vinegar
• 1 tablespoon Dijon mustard
• Salt and pepper to taste

Instructions:
1. Preheat your Traeger grill to 375°F.
2. Rub quail halves with olive oil and season with salt and pepper.
3. In a saucepan, combine cherry preserves, balsamic vinegar, Dijon mustard, salt, and pepper to make the cherry glaze.
4. Simmer the glaze over low heat until slightly thickened.
5. Place quail halves directly on the grill grate.
6. Smoke the quail for about 20-25 minutes, brushing with cherry glaze during the last 10 minutes of cooking.
7. Remove from the grill and let rest for a few minutes before serving.

Pheasant with Herb Butter
Prep Time: 20 minutes | Cooking Time: 25 minutes | Serves: 4

Ingredients:
• 2 pheasant breasts
• Olive oil
• Salt and pepper to taste

Herb butter:

• 4 tablespoons unsalted butter, softened
• 1 tablespoon chopped fresh herbs (such as thyme, rosemary, and sage)
• 1 garlic clove, minced
• Salt and pepper to taste

Instructions:
1. Preheat your Traeger grill to 400°F.
2. Rub pheasant breasts with olive oil and season with salt and pepper.
3. In a bowl, mix softened butter, chopped fresh herbs, minced garlic, salt, and pepper to make the herb butter.
4. Gently lift the skin of each pheasant breast and spread some herb butter underneath.
5. Place the pheasant breasts directly on the grill grate.
6. Grill the pheasant for about 10-12 minutes per side or until cooked through and juices run clear.
7. Remove from the grill and let rest for a few minutes before slicing and serving.

Cornish Game Hens with Rosemary Lemon Glaze
Prep Time: 20 minutes | Cooking Time: 1 hour | Serves: 2-4

Ingredients:
• 2 Cornish game hens
• Olive oil
• Salt and pepper to taste
• Fresh rosemary sprigs
• Lemon slices

Rosemary lemon glaze:
• Juice of 1 lemon
• Zest of 1 lemon
• 2 tablespoons honey
• 1 tablespoon Dijon mustard
• 1 teaspoon minced fresh rosemary
• Salt and pepper to taste

Instructions:
1. Preheat your Traeger grill to 375°F.
2. Rub Cornish game hens with olive oil and season inside and out with salt and pepper.
3. Stuff cavity of each hen with fresh rosemary sprigs and lemon slices.
4. Place the hens directly on the grill grate.
5. Smoke the hens for about 45-60 minutes, or until

the internal temperature reaches 165°F, brushing with rosemary lemon glaze during the last 15 minutes of cooking.

6. Remove from the grill and let rest for a few minutes before serving.

BBQ Turkey Meatballs
Prep Time: 20 minutes | Cooking Time: 30 minutes | Serves: 4

Ingredients:
- 1 pound ground turkey
- 1/4 cup breadcrumbs
- 1/4 cup grated Parmesan cheese
- 1 egg
- 1/4 cup BBQ sauce
- Salt and pepper to taste
- Olive oil
- Chopped fresh parsley for garnish

Instructions:
1. Preheat your Traeger grill to 375°F.
2. In a bowl, mix ground turkey, breadcrumbs, grated Parmesan, egg, BBQ sauce, salt, and pepper until well combined.
3. Form the mixture into meatballs of desired size.
4. Brush meatballs with olive oil and place them on a grill-safe pan or tray.
5. Grill the meatballs for about 25-30 minutes, turning occasionally, until cooked through and browned.
6. Remove from the grill and sprinkle with chopped fresh parsley before serving.

Smoked Pesto Chicken Thighs
Prep Time: 15 minutes | Cooking Time: 1 hour | Serves: 4

Ingredients:
- 4 chicken thighs, bone-in and skin-on
- Olive oil
- Salt and pepper to taste
- Pesto sauce (store-bought or homemade)
- Pine nuts for garnish (optional)

Instructions:
1. Preheat your Traeger grill to 375°F.
2. Rub chicken thighs with olive oil and season with salt and pepper.
3. Place the chicken thighs directly on the grill grate,

skin-side up.
4. Smoke the chicken thighs for about 45-60 minutes or until the internal temperature reaches 165°F.
5. Remove from the grill and let rest for a few minutes.
6. Brush chicken thighs with pesto sauce and sprinkle with pine nuts before serving.

Lemon Herb Turkey Burgers
Prep Time: 20 minutes | Cooking Time: 15 minutes | Serves: 4

Ingredients:
- 1 pound ground turkey
- 1/4 cup breadcrumbs
- 1/4 cup grated Parmesan cheese
- 1 egg
- Zest of 1 lemon
- 2 tablespoons chopped fresh herbs (such as parsley, thyme, and basil)
- Salt and pepper to taste
- Olive oil
- Burger buns and toppings of choice

Instructions:
1. Preheat your Traeger grill to 400°F.
2. In a bowl, mix ground turkey, breadcrumbs, grated Parmesan, egg, lemon zest, chopped herbs, salt, and pepper until well combined.
3. Divide the mixture into 4 equal portions and form into burger patties.
4. Brush burger patties with olive oil and place them on the grill grate.
5. Grill the turkey burgers for about 6-8 minutes per side or until cooked through and internal temperature reaches 165°F.
6. Toast burger buns on the grill during the last few minutes of cooking.
7. Assemble burgers with toppings of your choice and serve hot.

Honey Mustard Glazed Cornish Game Hens
Prep Time: 20 minutes | Cooking Time: 1 hour | Serves: 2-4

Ingredients:
- 2 Cornish game hens
- Olive oil
- Salt and pepper to taste
- Fresh herbs for garnish

Honey mustard glaze:
- 1/4 cup honey
- 2 tablespoons Dijon mustard
- 1 tablespoon apple cider vinegar
- 1 teaspoon minced garlic
- Salt and pepper to taste

Instructions:
1. Preheat your Traeger grill to 375°F.
2. Rub Cornish game hens with olive oil and season inside and out with salt and pepper.
3. In a bowl, mix honey, Dijon mustard, apple cider vinegar, minced garlic, salt, and pepper to make the honey mustard glaze.
4. Place the hens directly on the grill grate.
5. Smoke the hens for about 45 minutes, then brush with honey mustard glaze.
6. Continue smoking for another 15-20 minutes or until the internal temperature reaches 165°F and skin is golden and crispy.
7. Remove from the grill, let rest for a few minutes, then garnish with fresh herbs before serving.

Duck Tacos with Mango Salsa
Prep Time: 30 minutes | Cooking Time: 20 minutes | Serves: 4

Ingredients:
- 2 duck breasts
- Olive oil
- Salt and pepper to taste
- Corn or flour tortillas
- Mango salsa (store-bought or homemade)
- Fresh cilantro leaves for garnish
- Lime wedges for serving

Instructions:
1. In a bowl, marinate duck breasts with olive oil, salt, and pepper for at least 30 minutes.
2. Preheat your Traeger grill to medium-high heat.
3. Grill the duck breasts for about 6-8 minutes per side or until desired doneness (medium-rare to medium).
4. Remove from the grill and let rest for a few minutes before slicing thinly.
5. Warm tortillas on the grill for a few seconds.
6. Fill each tortilla with sliced duck breast, mango salsa, and fresh cilantro.
7. Serve the Traeger smoked duck tacos with lime

wedges on the side.

Lemon Garlic Chicken Wings
Prep Time: 15 minutes | Cooking Time: 45 minutes | Serves: 4-6

Ingredients:
- 2 pounds chicken wings
- Olive oil
- Salt and pepper to taste
- Zest of 1 lemon
- 2 tablespoons minced garlic
- Chopped fresh parsley for garnish

Instructions:
1. Preheat your Traeger grill to 375°F.
2. Toss chicken wings with olive oil, salt, pepper, lemon zest, and minced garlic until coated.
3. Place the wings on the grill grate.
4. Grill the chicken wings for about 40-45 minutes, turning occasionally, until golden and crispy.
5. Remove from the grill and sprinkle with chopped fresh parsley before serving.

Maple Glazed Chicken Drumsticks
Prep Time: 10 minutes | Cooking Time: 40 minutes | Serves: 4

Ingredients:
- 8 chicken drumsticks
- Olive oil
- Salt and pepper to taste

Maple glaze:
- 1/4 cup maple syrup
- 2 tablespoons soy sauce
- 1 tablespoon Dijon mustard
- 1 teaspoon minced garlic
- Salt and pepper to taste

Instructions:
1. Preheat your Traeger grill to 375°F.
2. Brush chicken drumsticks with olive oil and season with salt and pepper.
3. Place the drumsticks directly on the grill grate.
4. Grill the chicken drumsticks for about 30-35 minutes, turning occasionally, until cooked through and browned.
5. In a saucepan, combine maple syrup, soy sauce,

Dijon mustard, minced garlic, salt, and pepper to make the maple glaze.
6. Heat the glaze over medium heat until it thickens slightly.
7. Brush the grilled chicken drumsticks with the maple glaze during the last 10 minutes of cooking.
8. Remove from the grill and serve hot.

Chicken and Veggie Skewers

Prep Time: 20 minutes | Cooking Time: 15 minutes | Serves: 4

Ingredients:
- 2 boneless, skinless chicken breasts, cut into cubes
- 2 bell peppers, cut into chunks
- 1 red onion, cut into chunks
- Cherry tomatoes
- Olive oil
- Salt and pepper to taste
- Skewers

Instructions:
1. Preheat your Traeger grill to medium-high heat.
2. Thread chicken cubes, bell pepper chunks, red onion chunks, and cherry tomatoes onto skewers.
3. Brush skewers with olive oil and season with salt and pepper.
4. Grill the skewers for about 10-12 minutes, turning occasionally, until chicken is cooked through and vegetables are tender.
5. Remove from the grill and serve hot as a delicious and colorful meal.

Smoked Chicken Quesadillas

Prep Time: 20 minutes | Cooking Time: 15 minutes | Serves: 4

Ingredients:
- 2 boneless, skinless chicken breasts
- Olive oil
- Salt and pepper to taste
- Mexican seasoning blend
- Flour tortillas
- Shredded Mexican cheese blend
- Diced bell peppers and onions
- Salsa, sour cream, and guacamole for serving

Instructions:
1. Preheat your Traeger grill to 375°F.

2. Rub chicken breasts with olive oil and season with salt, pepper, and Mexican seasoning blend.
3. Place the chicken breasts directly on the grill grate.
4. Smoke the chicken breasts for about 20-25 minutes or until cooked through.
5. Remove from the grill and let rest for a few minutes before slicing into strips.
6. Heat a skillet on the grill or stovetop.
7. Place a flour tortilla in the skillet and sprinkle with shredded cheese.
8. Add sliced chicken, diced bell peppers, onions, and another layer of cheese on top.
9. Top with another tortilla and cook until the cheese is melted and tortilla is crispy, flipping once.
10. Remove from the skillet and cut into wedges.
11. Serve the Traeger smoked chicken quesadillas with salsa, sour cream, and guacamole.

Honey Sriracha Glazed Chicken Wings

Prep Time: 15 minutes | Cooking Time: 45 minutes | Serves: 4-6

Ingredients:
- 2 pounds chicken wings
- Olive oil
- Salt and pepper to taste

Honey Sriracha glaze:
1/4 cup honey
2 tablespoons Sriracha sauce
1 tablespoon soy sauce
1 teaspoon minced garlic
Salt and pepper to taste

Instructions:
1. Preheat your Traeger grill to 375°F.
2. Toss chicken wings with olive oil, salt, and pepper.
3. Place the wings on the grill grate.
4. Grill the chicken wings for about 40-45 minutes, turning occasionally, until golden and crispy.
5. In a saucepan, combine honey, Sriracha sauce, soy sauce, minced garlic, salt, and pepper to make the glaze.
6. Heat the glaze over medium heat until it thickens slightly.
7. Brush the grilled chicken wings with the honey Sriracha glaze during the last 10 minutes of cooking.
8. Remove from the grill and serve hot.

Chicken Alfredo Pasta

Prep Time: 20 minutes | Cooking Time: 30 minutes | Serves: 4

Ingredients:
- 2 boneless, skinless chicken breasts
- Olive oil
- Salt and pepper to taste
- Italian seasoning blend
- 8 ounces fettuccine pasta
- Alfredo sauce (store-bought or homemade)
- Grated Parmesan cheese for garnish
- Chopped fresh parsley for garnish

Instructions:
1. Preheat your Traeger grill to medium-high heat.
2. Rub chicken breasts with olive oil and season with salt, pepper, and Italian seasoning blend.
3. Place the chicken breasts directly on the grill grate.
4. Grill the chicken breasts for about 6-8 minutes per side or until cooked through.
5. Remove from the grill and let rest for a few minutes before slicing into strips.
6. Cook fettuccine pasta according to package instructions, drain, and set aside.
7. In a saucepan, heat Alfredo sauce until warm.
8. Toss cooked pasta with Alfredo sauce.
9. Arrange sliced chicken on top of the Alfredo pasta.
10. Sprinkle with grated Parmesan cheese and chopped fresh parsley before serving.

Chicken Caprese Salad

Prep Time: 15 minutes | Cooking Time: 15 minutes | Serves: 4

Ingredients:
- 2 boneless, skinless chicken breasts
- Olive oil
- Salt and pepper to taste
- Italian seasoning blend
- Fresh mozzarella cheese, sliced
- Cherry tomatoes, halved
- Fresh basil leaves
- Balsamic glaze
- Mixed salad greens

Instructions:
1. Preheat your Traeger grill to medium-high heat.
2. Rub chicken breasts with olive oil and season with salt, pepper, and Italian seasoning blend.
3. Place the chicken breasts directly on the grill grate.
4. Grill the chicken breasts for about 6-8 minutes per side or until cooked through.
5. Remove from the grill and let rest for a few minutes before slicing.
6. Arrange mixed salad greens on serving plates.
7. Top the greens with sliced grilled chicken, fresh mozzarella slices, cherry tomatoes, and fresh basil leaves.
8. Drizzle with balsamic glaze before serving.

Turkey Meatloaf

Prep Time: 20 minutes | Cooking Time: 1 hour | Serves: 6-8

Ingredients:
- 1 pound ground turkey
- 1 cup breadcrumbs
- 1/2 cup milk
- 1/2 cup grated Parmesan cheese
- 1/4 cup chopped fresh parsley
- 1/4 cup chopped onion
- 1/4 cup chopped bell pepper
- 2 cloves garlic, minced
- 1 egg
- Salt and pepper to taste
- BBQ sauce for glazing

Instructions:
1. Preheat your Traeger grill to 375°F.
2. In a bowl, mix ground turkey, breadcrumbs, milk, Parmesan cheese, parsley, onion, bell pepper, garlic, egg, salt, and pepper until well combined.
3. Shape the mixture into a loaf and place it on a grill-safe pan or tray.
4. Smoke the turkey meatloaf for about 45 minutes to 1 hour, brushing with BBQ sauce during the last 15 minutes of cooking.
5. Remove from the grill and let rest for a few minutes before slicing.

Lemon Garlic Chicken Kabobs

Prep Time: 20 minutes | Cooking Time: 10 minutes | Serves: 4

Ingredients:
- 1 pound chicken breast, cut into cubes
- Olive oil

- Salt and pepper to taste
- Zest and juice of 1 lemon
- 2 cloves garlic, minced
- Fresh rosemary sprigs
- Cherry tomatoes
- Red onion, cut into chunks
- Bell peppers, cut into chunks

Instructions:
1. In a bowl, mix olive oil, lemon zest, lemon juice, minced garlic, salt, and pepper.
2. Add chicken cubes to the marinade and let marinate in the refrigerator for at least 30 minutes.
3. Preheat your Traeger grill to medium-high heat.
4. Thread marinated chicken cubes, cherry tomatoes, red onion chunks, and bell pepper chunks onto skewers.
5. Grill the kabobs for about 8-10 minutes, turning occasionally, until chicken is cooked through and veggies are tender.
6. Remove from the grill and serve hot.

Honey Mustard Chicken Thighs
Prep Time: 10 minutes | Cooking Time: 30 minutes | Serves: 4

Ingredients:
- 4 chicken thighs, bone-in and skin-on
- Olive oil
- Salt and pepper to taste

Honey mustard sauce:
- 1/4 cup honey
- 2 tablespoons Dijon mustard
- 1 tablespoon apple cider vinegar
- 1 teaspoon minced garlic
- Salt and pepper to taste

Instructions:
1. Preheat your Traeger grill to 375°F.
2. Rub chicken thighs with olive oil and season with salt and pepper.
3. Place the chicken thighs directly on the grill grate, skin-side up.
4. Smoke the chicken thighs for about 20 minutes.
5. In a saucepan, combine honey, Dijon mustard, apple cider vinegar, minced garlic, salt, and pepper to make the honey mustard sauce.
6. Brush the chicken thighs with the honey mustard

sauce and continue smoking for another 10-15 minutes or until internal temperature reaches 165°F.
7. Remove from the grill and let rest for a few minutes before serving.

Chicken Pesto Flatbread
Prep Time: 15 minutes | Cooking Time: 10 minutes | Serves: 4

Ingredients:
- 2 boneless, skinless chicken breasts
- Olive oil
- Salt and pepper to taste
- Italian seasoning blend
- Flatbread or pizza crust
- Pesto sauce (store-bought or homemade)
- Shredded mozzarella cheese
- Cherry tomatoes, halved
- Fresh basil leaves

Instructions:
1. Preheat your Traeger grill to 400°F.
2. Rub chicken breasts with olive oil and season with salt, pepper, and Italian seasoning blend.
3. Place the chicken breasts directly on the grill grate.
4. Grill the chicken breasts for about 6-8 minutes per side or until cooked through.
5. Remove from the grill and let rest for a few minutes before slicing thinly.
6. Spread pesto sauce over flatbread or pizza crust.
7. Sprinkle shredded mozzarella cheese over the pesto.
8. Arrange sliced grilled chicken, cherry tomato halves, and fresh basil leaves on top.
9. Place the flatbread on the grill and cook for about 5-7 minutes or until cheese is melted and bubbly.
10. Remove from the grill, slice, and serve hot.

Chicken Alfredo Stuffed Peppers
Prep Time: 20 minutes | Cooking Time: 30 minutes | Serves: 4

Ingredients:
- 4 large bell peppers, halved and seeds removed
- Olive oil
- Salt and pepper to taste
- 1 cup cooked chicken breast, shredded
- Alfredo sauce (store-bought or homemade)
- Cooked pasta (penne or fettuccine)
- Grated Parmesan cheese

• Chopped fresh parsley for garnish

Instructions:
1. Preheat your Traeger grill to 375°F.
2. Brush bell pepper halves with olive oil and season with salt and pepper.
3. Place the bell pepper halves directly on the grill grate, cut-side down.
4. Smoke the peppers for about 15-20 minutes or until slightly softened.
5. In a bowl, mix shredded chicken with Alfredo sauce and cooked pasta.
6. Fill each bell pepper half with the chicken Alfredo mixture.
7. Sprinkle grated Parmesan cheese over the stuffed peppers.
8. Place the stuffed peppers back on the grill and smoke for another 10-15 minutes.
9. Remove from the grill, garnish with chopped fresh parsley, and serve hot.

Chicken Teriyaki Rice Bowl
Prep Time: 20 minutes | Cooking Time: 20 minutes | Serves: 4

Ingredients:
• 2 boneless, skinless chicken breasts
• Olive oil
• Salt and pepper to taste
• Teriyaki marinade or sauce
• Cooked white or brown rice
• Sliced cucumbers
• Sliced carrots
• Sliced avocado
• Sesame seeds for garnish

Instructions:
1. In a bowl, mix olive oil, salt, pepper, and teriyaki marinade.
2. Add chicken breasts to the marinade and let marinate in the refrigerator for at least 30 minutes.
3. Preheat your Traeger grill to medium-high heat.
4. Grill the marinated chicken breasts for about 6-8 minutes per side or until cooked through.
5. Remove from the grill and let rest for a few minutes before slicing.
6. Assemble rice bowls with cooked rice, sliced grilled chicken, sliced cucumbers, carrots, and avocado.
7. Drizzle with extra teriyaki sauce and sprinkle with

sesame seeds before serving.

Chicken Tikka Masala
Prep Time: 30 minutes | Cooking Time: 1 hour | Serves: 4-6

Ingredients:
• 2 pounds chicken thighs, boneless and skinless, cut into cubes
• Olive oil
• Salt and pepper to taste
• Chopped fresh cilantro for garnish
• Cooked basmati rice or naan bread for serving

Tikka masala marinade:
1 cup plain yogurt
2 tablespoons tomato paste
2 tablespoons lemon juice
2 teaspoons minced garlic
2 teaspoons grated ginger
2 teaspoons garam masala
1 teaspoon ground cumin
1 teaspoon paprika
1/2 teaspoon turmeric
1/2 teaspoon cayenne pepper

Instructions:
1. In a bowl, mix yogurt, tomato paste, lemon juice, minced garlic, grated ginger, garam masala, ground cumin, paprika, turmeric, cayenne pepper, salt, and pepper to make the tikka masala marinade.
2. Add chicken cubes to the marinade and let marinate in the refrigerator for at least 2 hours or overnight.
3. Preheat your Traeger grill to 400°F.
4. Thread marinated chicken cubes onto skewers.
5. Grill the chicken skewers for about 10-15 minutes, turning occasionally, until chicken is cooked through and slightly charred.
6. In a saucepan, heat any remaining marinade until it simmers and thickens slightly.
7. Remove chicken from skewers and place in a serving dish.
8. Pour the simmered marinade over the chicken.
9. Garnish with chopped fresh cilantro.
10. Serve the Traeger smoked chicken tikka masala with basmati rice or naan bread.

Grilled Chicken and Veggie Wraps

Prep Time: 20 minutes | Cooking Time: 10 minutes | Serves: 4

Ingredients:
- 2 boneless, skinless chicken breasts
- Olive oil
- Salt and pepper to taste
- Cajun seasoning blend
- Flour tortillas or wraps
- Hummus or tzatziki sauce
- Sliced cucumber
- Sliced red onion
- Sliced tomato
- Fresh spinach leaves

Instructions:
1. Preheat your Traeger grill to medium-high heat.
2. Rub chicken breasts with olive oil and season with salt, pepper, and Cajun seasoning blend.
3. Place the chicken breasts directly on the grill grate.
4. Grill the chicken breasts for about 6-8 minutes per side or until cooked through.
5. Remove from the grill and let rest for a few minutes before slicing.
6. Spread hummus or tzatziki sauce over flour tortillas or wraps.
7. Arrange sliced grilled chicken, cucumber, red onion, tomato, and spinach on each tortilla.
8. Roll up the wraps and secure with toothpicks if needed.
9. Place the wraps on the grill for a few minutes to warm through.
10. Remove from the grill, slice diagonally, and serve hot.

Traeger Smoked Chicken Enchiladas

Prep Time: 30 minutes | Cooking Time: 30 minutes | Serves: 4-6

Ingredients:
- 2 boneless, skinless chicken breasts
- Olive oil
- Salt and pepper to taste
- 1 onion, chopped
- 2 cloves garlic, minced
- 1 can (10 ounces) enchilada sauce
- 1 can (4 ounces) chopped green chilies
- 1 cup shredded Mexican cheese blend
- 8 flour or corn tortillas

- Chopped fresh cilantro for garnish
- Sour cream and sliced avocado for serving

Instructions:
1. Preheat your Traeger grill to 375°F.
2. Rub chicken breasts with olive oil and season with salt and pepper.
3. Place the chicken breasts directly on the grill grate.
4. Smoke the chicken breasts for about 20-25 minutes or until cooked through.
5. Remove from the grill and let cool slightly before shredding.
6. In a skillet, sauté chopped onion and minced garlic until softened.
7. Add shredded chicken, enchilada sauce, chopped green chilies, and half of the shredded cheese to the skillet.
8. Cook until heated through and cheese is melted.
9. Warm tortillas on the grill for a few seconds.
10. Spoon chicken mixture onto each tortilla, roll up, and place seam-side down in a baking dish.
11. Pour remaining enchilada sauce over the rolled tortillas and sprinkle with the remaining shredded cheese.
12. Place the baking dish on the grill and bake for about 10-15 minutes or until cheese is bubbly.
13. Remove from the grill, garnish with chopped fresh cilantro, and serve with sour cream and sliced avocado.

Smoked Chicken and Mushroom Risotto

Prep Time: 15 minutes | Cooking Time: 45 minutes | Serves: 4

Ingredients:
- 2 boneless, skinless chicken thighs
- Olive oil
- Salt and pepper to taste
- 1 cup Arborio rice
- 4 cups chicken broth
- 1/2 cup white wine (optional)
- 1 cup sliced mushrooms
- 1/2 cup grated Parmesan cheese
- Chopped fresh parsley for garnish

Instructions:
1. Preheat your Traeger grill to 375°F.
2. Rub chicken thighs with olive oil and season with salt and pepper.
3. Place the chicken thighs directly on the grill grate.

4. Smoke the chicken thighs for about 30-35 minutes or until cooked through.
5. Remove from the grill and let rest for a few minutes before slicing into strips.
6. In a large saucepan, heat olive oil over medium heat.
7. Add Arborio rice and cook, stirring, for about 1 minute.
8. Pour in white wine and cook until evaporated.
9. Gradually add chicken broth, 1/2 cup at a time, stirring constantly until absorbed before adding more.
10. Stir in sliced mushrooms and continue cooking until rice is creamy and tender.
11. Remove from heat and stir in grated Parmesan cheese.
12. Serve the smoked chicken and mushroom risotto hot, garnished with chopped fresh parsley.

Grilled Chicken Shawarma Wraps

Prep Time: 30 minutes | Cooking Time: 10 minutes | Serves: 4

Ingredients:
- 2 boneless, skinless chicken breasts
- Olive oil
- Salt and pepper to taste
- Flatbread or pita wraps
- Sliced cucumbers
- Sliced tomatoes
- Sliced red onions
- Tzatziki sauce for serving

Shawarma marinade:
- 1/4 cup plain yogurt
- 2 tablespoons olive oil
- 2 tablespoons lemon juice
- 1 tablespoon ground cumin
- 1 tablespoon ground coriander
- 1 teaspoon paprika
- 1 teaspoon ground turmeric
- 1 teaspoon minced garlic
- Salt and pepper to taste

Instructions:
1. In a bowl, mix yogurt, olive oil, lemon juice, ground cumin, ground coriander, paprika, turmeric, minced garlic, salt, and pepper to make the shawarma marinade.
2. Add chicken breasts to the marinade and let marinate in the refrigerator for at least 2 hours or overnight.
3. Preheat your Traeger grill to medium-high heat.
4. Grill the marinated chicken breasts for about 6-8 minutes per side or until cooked through.
5. Remove from the grill and let rest for a few minutes before slicing thinly.
6. Warm flatbread or pita wraps on the grill for a few seconds.
7. Spread tzatziki sauce over each flatbread.
8. Arrange sliced grilled chicken, cucumbers, tomatoes, and red onions on each wrap.
9. Roll up the wraps and secure with toothpicks if needed.
10. Place the wraps back on the grill for a few minutes to warm through.
11. Remove from the grill, slice diagonally, and serve hot.

Smoked Chicken and Corn Chowder

Prep Time: 20 minutes | Cooking Time: 1 hour | Serves: 6

Ingredients:
- 2 boneless, skinless chicken breasts
- Olive oil
- Salt and pepper to taste
- 4 slices bacon, chopped
- 1 onion, chopped
- 2 cloves garlic, minced
- 2 potatoes, peeled and diced
- 2 cups fresh or frozen corn kernels
- 4 cups chicken broth
- 1 cup heavy cream
- Chopped fresh parsley for garnish

Instructions:
1. Preheat your Traeger grill to 375°F.
2. Rub chicken breasts with olive oil and season with salt and pepper.
3. Place the chicken breasts directly on the grill grate.
4. Smoke the chicken breasts for about 30-35 minutes or until cooked through.
5. Remove from the grill and let rest for a few minutes before chopping into bite-sized pieces.
6. In a large pot, cook chopped bacon until crispy.
7. Add chopped onion and minced garlic to the pot and cook until softened.
8. Stir in diced potatoes and corn kernels.
9. Pour in chicken broth and bring to a boil.

10. Reduce heat and simmer until potatoes are tender.
11. Stir in chopped smoked chicken and heavy cream.
12. Simmer for another 10-15 minutes.
13. Season with salt and pepper to taste.
14. Serve the Traeger smoked chicken and corn chowder hot, garnished with chopped fresh parsley.

Grilled Chicken and Asparagus Stir-Fry

Prep Time: 20 minutes | **Cooking Time:** 10 minutes | **Serves:** 4

Ingredients:
- 2 boneless, skinless chicken thighs
- Olive oil
- Salt and pepper to taste
- 1 bunch asparagus, trimmed and cut into pieces
- 1 red bell pepper, sliced
- 1 yellow bell pepper, sliced
- 1/2 onion, sliced
- 2 cloves garlic, minced
- Soy sauce
- Sesame oil
- Cooked rice for serving

Instructions:
1. Preheat your Traeger grill to medium-high heat.
2. Rub chicken thighs with olive oil and season with salt and pepper.
3. Place the chicken thighs directly on the grill grate.
4. Grill the chicken thighs for about 6-8 minutes per side or until cooked through.
5. Remove from the grill and let rest for a few minutes before slicing into strips.
6. Heat a skillet on the grill or stovetop.
7. Add a little olive oil to the skillet and sauté minced garlic until fragrant.
8. Add sliced bell peppers, onion, and asparagus to the skillet.
9. Stir-fry the vegetables until tender-crisp.
10. Add sliced grilled chicken to the skillet.
11. Drizzle with soy sauce and sesame oil to taste.
12. Stir-fry everything together for a few more minutes.
13. Serve the Traeger grilled chicken and asparagus stir-fry over cooked rice.

Smoked Chicken Pesto Pasta

Prep Time: 20 minutes | **Cooking Time:** 30 minutes | **Serves:** 4

Ingredients:
- 2 boneless, skinless chicken breasts
- Olive oil
- Salt and pepper to taste
- Italian seasoning blend
- 8 ounces penne pasta
- Pesto sauce (store-bought or homemade)
- Cherry tomatoes, halved
- Grated Parmesan cheese for garnish
- Chopped fresh basil for garnish

Instructions:
1. Preheat your Traeger grill to medium-high heat.
2. Rub chicken breasts with olive oil and season with salt, pepper, and Italian seasoning blend.
3. Place the chicken breasts directly on the grill grate.
4. Grill the chicken breasts for about 6-8 minutes per side or until cooked through.
5. Remove from the grill and let rest for a few minutes before slicing thinly.
6. Cook penne pasta according to package instructions, drain, and set aside.
7. In a large bowl, toss cooked pasta with pesto sauce.
8. Add halved cherry tomatoes and sliced grilled chicken to the pasta.
9. Mix everything together until well combined.
10. Serve the Traeger smoked chicken pesto pasta hot, garnished with grated Parmesan cheese and chopped fresh basil.

Grilled Chicken and Avocado Sandwiches

Prep Time: 15 minutes | **Cooking Time:** 10 minutes | **Serves:** 4

Ingredients:
- 2 boneless, skinless chicken breasts
- Olive oil
- Salt and pepper to taste
- Cajun seasoning blend
- Ciabatta rolls or sandwich buns
- Romaine lettuce leaves
- Sliced tomatoes
- Sliced avocado
- Spicy mayo (mayonnaise mixed with hot sauce)
- Sliced red onion (optional)

Instructions:
1. Preheat your Traeger grill to medium-high heat.
2. Rub chicken breasts with olive oil and season with salt, pepper, and Cajun seasoning blend.
3. Place the chicken breasts directly on the grill grate.
4. Grill the chicken breasts for about 6-8 minutes per side or until cooked through.
5. Remove from the grill and let rest for a few minutes before slicing.
6. Slice ciabatta rolls or sandwich buns in half.
7. Spread spicy mayo on the bottom halves of the rolls.
8. Layer romaine lettuce leaves, sliced tomatoes, sliced avocado, and grilled chicken on the rolls.
9. Add sliced red onion if desired.
10. Cover with the top halves of the rolls.
11. Grill the sandwiches on the grill for a few minutes on each side until toasted and heated through.
12. Remove from the grill, slice in half if desired, and serve hot.

Smoked Chicken Tacos with Mango Salsa

Prep Time: 30 minutes | Cooking Time: 15 minutes | Serves: 4

Ingredients:
- 2 boneless, skinless chicken thighs
- Olive oil
- Salt and pepper to taste
- Taco seasoning blend
- Flour or corn tortillas
- Shredded cabbage or lettuce
- Sliced radishes for garnish
- Lime wedges for serving

Mango salsa:
- 1 ripe mango, diced
- 1/2 red onion, diced
- 1/4 cup chopped fresh cilantro
- Juice of 1 lime
- Salt and pepper to taste

Instructions:
1. In a bowl, mix olive oil, salt, pepper, and taco seasoning blend.
2. Add chicken thighs to the marinade and let marinate in the refrigerator for at least 2 hours or overnight.
3. Preheat your Traeger grill to medium-high heat.
4. Grill the marinated chicken thighs for about 6-8

minutes per side or until cooked through.
5. Remove from the grill and let rest for a few minutes before slicing thinly.
6. Warm flour or corn tortillas on the grill for a few seconds on each side.
7. In a bowl, combine diced mango, diced red onion, chopped cilantro, lime juice, salt, and pepper to make the mango salsa.
8. Assemble tacos by placing shredded cabbage or lettuce on each tortilla.
9. Top with sliced grilled chicken, mango salsa, and sliced radishes.
10. Serve the Traeger smoked chicken tacos with lime wedges for squeezing.

Grilled Chicken Pita Pockets with Greek Salad

Prep Time: 30 minutes | Cooking Time: 10 minutes | Serves: 4

Ingredients:
- 2 boneless, skinless chicken breasts
- Olive oil
- Salt and pepper to taste

Greek marinade:
- 1/4 cup plain yogurt
- 2 tablespoons olive oil
- 2 tablespoons lemon juice
- 1 teaspoon dried oregano
- 1 teaspoon minced garlic
- Salt and pepper to taste
- Pita pockets

Greek salad:
- Chopped cucumbers
- Chopped tomatoes
- Sliced red onions
- Kalamata olives
- Crumbled feta cheese
- Chopped fresh parsley
- Greek dressing

Instructions:
1. In a bowl, mix yogurt, olive oil, lemon juice, dried oregano, minced garlic, salt, and pepper to make the Greek marinade.
2. Add chicken breasts to the marinade and let marinate in the refrigerator for at least 2 hours or

overnight.

3. Preheat your Traeger grill to medium-high heat.

4. Grill the marinated chicken breasts for about 6-8 minutes per side or until cooked through.

5. Remove from the grill and let rest for a few minutes before slicing thinly.

6. Cut pita pockets in half to form pockets.

7. Fill each pita pocket with sliced grilled chicken and Greek salad ingredients.

8. Drizzle Greek dressing over the fillings.

9. Serve the Traeger grilled chicken pita pockets with Greek salad immediately.

Chicken and Spinach Stuffed Portobello Mushrooms

Prep Time: 20 minutes | Cooking Time: 20 minutes | Serves: 4

Ingredients:
- 4 large portobello mushrooms, stems removed
- Olive oil
- Salt and pepper to taste
- 2 boneless, skinless chicken breasts
- Italian seasoning blend
- Fresh spinach leaves
- Shredded mozzarella cheese
- Grated Parmesan cheese
- Chopped fresh parsley for garnish

Instructions:
1. Preheat your Traeger grill to 375°F.

2. Brush portobello mushrooms with olive oil and season with salt and pepper.

3. Place the mushrooms directly on the grill grate, gill-side up.

4. Smoke the mushrooms for about 10 minutes.

5. Rub chicken breasts with olive oil and season with salt, pepper, and Italian seasoning blend.

6. Place the chicken breasts directly on the grill grate.

7. Grill the chicken breasts for about 6-8 minutes per side or until cooked through.

8. Remove from the grill and let rest for a few minutes before slicing thinly.

9. Fill each smoked mushroom with fresh spinach leaves.

10. Top with sliced grilled chicken, shredded mozzarella cheese, and grated Parmesan cheese.

11. Place the stuffed mushrooms back on the grill and smoke for another 10 minutes or until cheese is melted and bubbly.

12. Remove from the grill, garnish with chopped fresh parsley, and serve hot.

Chapter 7: Beef, Pork, Lamb

Beef Tenderloin with Herb Butter

Prep Time: 15 minutes | Cooking Time: 20 minutes | Serves: 4-6

Ingredients:
- 2 pounds beef tenderloin
- Olive oil
- Salt and pepper to taste
- 1 tablespoon minced garlic
- 2 tablespoons chopped fresh herbs

Herb butter:
- 1/2 cup unsalted butter, softened
- 2 tablespoons chopped fresh herbs
- Salt and pepper to taste

Instructions:
1. Rub beef tenderloin with olive oil and season with salt, pepper, minced garlic, and chopped fresh herbs.
2. Let the beef tenderloin marinate in the refrigerator for at least 2 hours or overnight.
3. Preheat your Traeger grill to high heat.
4. Grill the marinated beef tenderloin for about 8-10 minutes per side or until desired doneness (medium-rare, medium, or well-done).
5. Remove from the grill and let rest for a few minutes before slicing.
6. In a small bowl, mix softened butter with chopped fresh herbs, salt, and pepper to make herb butter.
7. Serve sliced beef tenderloin with a dollop of herb butter on top.

Pork Ribs with BBQ Sauce

Prep Time: 15 minutes | Cooking Time: 4 hours | Serves: 4-6

Ingredients:
- 2 racks of pork ribs
- Olive oil
- Salt and pepper to taste
- BBQ rub
- BBQ sauce

Instructions:
1. Remove the membrane from the back of the pork ribs.
2. Rub ribs with olive oil and season with salt, pepper, and BBQ rub.
3. Let the ribs marinate in the refrigerator for at least 2

hours or overnight.
4. Preheat your Traeger grill to 225°F.
5. Place the marinated ribs directly on the grill grate, bone-side down.
6. Smoke the ribs for about 3-4 hours or until tender, basting with BBQ sauce every hour.
7. Increase the grill temperature to 375°F.
8. Grill the ribs for an additional 15-20 minutes to caramelize the BBQ sauce.
9. Remove from the grill, let rest for a few minutes, then slice and serve hot.

Beef Kebabs with Vegetables

Prep Time: 30 minutes | Cooking Time: 15 minutes | Serves: 4

Ingredients:
- 1 pound beef sirloin, cut into cubes
- Olive oil
- Salt and pepper to taste
- BBQ marinade or sauce (store-bought or homemade)
- Bell peppers, onions, cherry tomatoes (cut into chunks)
- Wooden skewers, soaked in water

Instructions:
1. In a bowl, mix beef cubes with olive oil, salt, pepper, and BBQ marinade.
2. Let the beef marinate in the refrigerator for at least 2 hours or overnight.
3. Preheat your Traeger grill to medium-high heat.
4. Thread marinated beef cubes and vegetable chunks onto soaked wooden skewers.
5. Grill the beef kebabs for about 10-15 minutes, turning occasionally, until beef is cooked to desired doneness and vegetables are tender.
6. Remove from the grill and serve hot.

Pork Shoulder with Carolina Mustard Sauce

Prep Time: 20 minutes | Cooking Time: 8 hours | Serves: 8-10

Ingredients:
- 5-6 pounds pork shoulder (pork butt)
- Olive oil
- Salt and pepper to taste
- Pork rub

Carolina mustard sauce:
- 1 cup yellow mustard
- 1/2 cup apple cider vinegar
- 1/4 cup honey
- 1/4 cup brown sugar
- 2 tablespoons Worcestershire sauce
- 1 tablespoon hot sauce
- 1 teaspoon garlic powder
- 1 teaspoon onion powder
- Salt and pepper to taste

Instructions:

1. Rub pork shoulder with olive oil and season with salt, pepper, and pork rub.
2. Let the pork shoulder marinate in the refrigerator for at least 4 hours or overnight.
3. Preheat your Traeger grill to 225°F.
4. Place the marinated pork shoulder directly on the grill grate, fat-side up.
5. Smoke the pork shoulder for about 6-8 hours, maintaining a consistent temperature.
6. In a saucepan, combine all ingredients for Carolina mustard sauce.
7. Simmer the sauce over low heat for about 10-15 minutes, stirring occasionally.
8. After smoking, wrap the pork shoulder in foil and let rest for 30 minutes.
9. Shred the smoked pork shoulder using forks or meat claws.
10. Serve the pulled pork with Carolina mustard sauce on the side.

Steak Fajitas

Prep Time: 30 minutes | Cooking Time: 15 minutes | Serves: 4-6

Ingredients:
- 1 pound skirt steak or flank steak
- Olive oil
- Salt and pepper to taste
- Bell peppers, onions (sliced)
- Flour or corn tortillas
- Salsa, guacamole, sour cream (for serving)

Fajita marinade:
- 1/4 cup olive oil
- 2 tablespoons lime juice
- 2 cloves garlic, minced
- 1 teaspoon ground cumin

- 1 teaspoon chili powder
- 1/2 teaspoon smoked paprika
- Salt and pepper to taste

Instructions:

1. In a bowl, mix olive oil, lime juice, minced garlic, ground cumin, chili powder, smoked paprika, salt, and pepper to make the fajita marinade.
2. Add skirt steak or flank steak to the marinade and let marinate in the refrigerator for at least 2 hours or overnight.
3. Preheat your Traeger grill to medium-high heat.
4. Grill the marinated steak for about 4-5 minutes per side or until cooked to desired doneness.
5. Remove from the grill and let rest for a few minutes before slicing thinly against the grain.
6. In a skillet, sauté sliced bell peppers and onions until tender.
7. Warm tortillas on the grill for a few seconds on each side.
8. Fill tortillas with sliced grilled steak, sautéed peppers, and onions.
9. Serve the Traeger grilled steak fajitas with salsa, guacamole, sour cream, and other desired toppings.

BBQ Meatloaf

Prep Time: 20 minutes | Cooking Time: 2 hours | Serves: 6-8

Ingredients:
- 2 pounds ground beef
- 1 onion, finely chopped
- 2 cloves garlic, minced
- 1/2 cup breadcrumbs
- 2 eggs
- 1/4 cup BBQ sauce (plus extra for topping)
- Salt and pepper to taste
- BBQ rub (store-bought or homemade)

Instructions:

1. In a bowl, combine ground beef, chopped onion, minced garlic, breadcrumbs, eggs, 1/4 cup BBQ sauce, salt, and pepper.
2. Mix everything together until well combined.
3. Shape the meat mixture into a loaf shape.
4. Preheat your Traeger grill to 225°F.
5. Place the meatloaf directly on the grill grate.
6. Smoke the meatloaf for about 1.5 to 2 hours or until internal temperature reaches 160°F.

7. Brush the top of the meatloaf with additional BBQ sauce during the last 30 minutes of cooking.

8. Remove from the grill, let rest for a few minutes, then slice and serve.

Beef and Veggie Skewers with Chimichurri Sauce

Prep Time: 30 minutes | Cooking Time: 15 minutes | Serves: 4

Ingredients:
- 1 pound beef sirloin, cut into cubes
- Olive oil
- Salt and pepper to taste
- Bell peppers, onions, mushrooms
- Wooden skewers, soaked in water

Chimichurri sauce:
- 1 cup fresh parsley, chopped
- 1/2 cup fresh cilantro, chopped
- 3 cloves garlic, minced
- 1/4 cup red wine vinegar
- 1/2 cup olive oil
- 1 teaspoon dried oregano
- Salt and pepper to taste

Instructions:
1. In a bowl, mix beef cubes with olive oil, salt, and pepper.
2. Let the beef marinate in the refrigerator for at least 2 hours or overnight.
3. Preheat your Traeger grill to medium-high heat.
4. Thread marinated beef cubes and vegetable chunks onto soaked wooden skewers.
5. Grill the beef and veggie skewers for about 10-15 minutes, turning occasionally, until beef is cooked to desired doneness and vegetables are tender.
6. In a blender or food processor, combine chopped parsley, chopped cilantro, minced garlic, red wine vinegar, olive oil, dried oregano, salt, and pepper to make chimichurri sauce.
7. Serve the grilled beef and veggie skewers with chimichurri sauce drizzled on top.

Pork Tenderloin with Apple Glaze

Prep Time: 15 minutes | Cooking Time: 1 hour | Serves: 4-6

Ingredients:

- 2 pounds pork tenderloin
- Olive oil
- Salt and pepper to taste
- Pork rub (store-bought or homemade)

Apple glaze:
- 1/2 cup apple juice
- 2 tablespoons honey
- 1 tablespoon Dijon mustard
- 1/2 teaspoon ground cinnamon
- Salt and pepper to taste

Instructions:
1. Rub pork tenderloin with olive oil and season with salt, pepper, and pork rub.
2. Let the pork tenderloin marinate in the refrigerator for at least 2 hours or overnight.
3. Preheat your Traeger grill to 375°F.
4. Place the marinated pork tenderloin directly on the grill grate.
5. Smoke the pork tenderloin for about 45 minutes to 1 hour or until internal temperature reaches 145°F.
6. In a saucepan, combine apple juice, honey, Dijon mustard, ground cinnamon, salt, and pepper to make apple glaze.
7. Simmer the glaze over low heat for about 10-15 minutes, stirring occasionally.
8. Brush the smoked pork tenderloin with apple glaze during the last 15 minutes of cooking.
9. Remove from the grill, let rest for a few minutes, then slice and serve.

Korean BBQ Beef Short Ribs

Prep Time: 30 minutes | Cooking Time: 15 minutes | Serves: 4

Ingredients:
2 pounds beef short ribs
Olive oil
Salt and pepper to taste

Korean BBQ marinade:
- 1/4 cup soy sauce
- 2 tablespoons brown sugar
- 2 tablespoons sesame oil
- 2 tablespoons rice vinegar
- 2 cloves garlic, minced
- 1 tablespoon grated ginger
- 1 tablespoon gochujang (Korean chili paste)

- 1 green onion, chopped
- Sesame seeds for garnish

Instructions:

1. In a bowl, mix soy sauce, brown sugar, sesame oil, rice vinegar, minced garlic, grated ginger, gochujang, and chopped green onion to make the Korean BBQ marinade.
2. Place beef short ribs in a shallow dish and pour the marinade over them, turning to coat evenly.
3. Let the beef short ribs marinate in the refrigerator for at least 4 hours or overnight.
4. Preheat your Traeger grill to medium-high heat.
5. Grill the marinated beef short ribs for about 5-7 minutes per side or until cooked to desired doneness.
6. Remove from the grill and let rest for a few minutes before slicing.
7. Sprinkle sliced beef short ribs with sesame seeds before serving.

Pulled Pork Sandwiches

Prep Time: 20 minutes | Cooking Time: 8 hours | Serves: 6-8

Ingredients:
- 5-6 pounds pork shoulder
- Olive oil
- Salt and pepper to taste
- Pork rub
- Coleslaw
- BBQ sauce
- Sandwich buns

Instructions:

1. Rub pork shoulder with olive oil and season with salt, pepper, and pork rub.
2. Let the pork shoulder marinate in the refrigerator for at least 4 hours or overnight.
3. Preheat your Traeger grill to 225°F.
4. Place the marinated pork shoulder directly on the grill grate, fat-side up.
5. Smoke the pork shoulder for about 6-8 hours, maintaining a consistent temperature.
6. After smoking, wrap the pork shoulder in foil and let rest for 30 minutes.
7. Shred the smoked pork shoulder using forks or meat claws.
8. Toss shredded pork with BBQ sauce.
9. Toast sandwich buns on the grill for a few minutes.

10. Fill toasted buns with pulled pork and top with coleslaw.
11. Serve the Traeger smoked pulled pork sandwiches hot.

Beef Tenderloin with Red Wine Reduction

Prep Time: 15 minutes | Cooking Time: 20 minutes | Serves: 4-6

Ingredients:
- 2 pounds beef tenderloin
- Olive oil
- Salt and pepper to taste
- Red wine
- Beef broth
- Shallots, minced
- Butter

Instructions:

1. Rub beef tenderloin with olive oil and season with salt and pepper.
2. Let it marinate for at least 2 hours.
3. Preheat Traeger grill to high heat.
4. Grill the tenderloin for about 6-8 minutes per side for medium-rare.
5. In a saucepan, sauté minced shallots in butter.
6. Add red wine and beef broth, simmer until reduced.
7. Slice the grilled beef tenderloin and serve with the red wine reduction.

Pork Belly Burnt Ends

Prep Time: 20 minutes | Cooking Time: 4 hours | Serves: 4-6

Ingredients:
- Pork belly, cubed
- BBQ rub
- BBQ sauce
- Brown sugar
- Butter

Instructions:

1. Rub pork belly cubes with BBQ rub and brown sugar.
2. Smoke on Traeger grill at 250°F for 3 hours.
3. Remove, toss with BBQ sauce and butter.
4. Return to grill for another hour or until caramelized.

5. Serve these savory burnt ends as a delicious appetizer or main dish.

Beef and Mushroom Skewers
Prep Time: 30 minutes | **Cooking Time:** 15 minutes | **Serves:** 4

Ingredients:
- Beef sirloin, cubed
- Mushrooms, whole or halved
- Olive oil
- Garlic powder
- Salt and pepper to taste

Instructions:
1. Marinate beef cubes in olive oil, garlic powder, salt, and pepper.
2. Thread beef and mushrooms onto skewers.
3. Grill on Traeger until beef is cooked and mushrooms are tender.
4. Serve these flavorful skewers as a main course or appetizer.

Pork Loin with Maple Glaze
Prep Time: 15 minutes | **Cooking Time:** 1.5 hours | **Serves:** 4-6

Ingredients:
- Pork loin
- Olive oil
- Salt and pepper to taste
- Maple syrup
- Dijon mustard
- Garlic, minced
- Thyme, chopped

Instructions:
1. Rub pork loin with olive oil, salt, and pepper.
2. Smoke on Traeger grill at 275°F.
3. Mix maple syrup, Dijon mustard, minced garlic, and thyme for glaze.
4. Brush glaze on pork loin during the last 30 minutes of smoking.
5. Let rest before slicing and serving with extra glaze.

Korean BBQ Beef Tacos
Prep Time: 30 minutes | **Cooking Time:** 15 minutes | **Serves:** 4

Ingredients:
- Beef short ribs, bone-in
- Soy sauce
- Brown sugar
- Sesame oil
- Garlic, minced
- Ginger, grated
- Corn tortillas
- Kimchi, for serving

Instructions:
1. Marinate short ribs in soy sauce, brown sugar, sesame oil, garlic, and ginger.
2. Grill on Traeger until charred and cooked.
3. Slice meat off the bone and serve in corn tortillas with kimchi.

Pork Chops with Apple Compote
Prep Time: 20 minutes | **Cooking Time:** 1 hour | **Serves:** 4

Ingredients:
- Pork chops
- Olive oil
- Salt and pepper to taste
- Apples, peeled and sliced
- Brown sugar
- Cinnamon
- Nutmeg

Instructions:
1. Rub pork chops with olive oil, salt, and pepper.
2. Smoke on Traeger grill at 275°F.
3. Sauté apples with brown sugar, cinnamon, and nutmeg until soft.
4. Serve smoked pork chops with apple compote on top.

Beef and Veggie Stir-Fry

Prep Time: 20 minutes | Cooking Time: 15 minutes | Serves: 4

Ingredients:
- Beef sirloin, thinly sliced
- Bell peppers, sliced
- Onion, sliced
- Broccoli florets
- Soy sauce
- Sesame oil
- Garlic, minced
- Ginger, grated
- Rice, for serving

Instructions:
1. Marinate beef slices in soy sauce, sesame oil, garlic, and ginger.
2. Grill beef on Traeger until cooked.
3. Stir-fry veggies in a hot pan with a splash of soy sauce.
4. Add grilled beef and toss.
5. Serve over cooked rice for a delicious meal.

Pulled Beef Sandwiches

Prep Time: 20 minutes | Cooking Time: 8 hours | Serves: 6-8

Ingredients:
- Beef chuck roast
- BBQ rub
- Beef broth
- BBQ sauce
- Sandwich buns

Instructions:
1. Rub chuck roast with BBQ rub and let it marinate.
2. Smoke on Traeger grill at 225°F until tender.
3. Shred the beef and mix with BBQ sauce and beef broth.
4. Serve on buns for delicious pulled beef sandwiches.

Pork Carnitas Tacos

Prep Time: 30 minutes | Cooking Time: 4 hours | Serves: 4

Ingredients:
- Pork shoulder, cubed
- Orange juice
- Lime juice
- Cumin
- Chili powder
- Onion, chopped
- Cilantro, chopped
- Corn tortillas

Instructions:
1. Marinate pork cubes in orange juice, lime juice, cumin, and chili powder.
2. Grill on Traeger until tender and slightly charred.
3. Sauté onions and cilantro.
4. Serve grilled pork in corn tortillas with onion and cilantro mix.

Traeger Smoked Beef Brisket with Coffee Rub

Prep Time: 30 minutes | Cooking Time: 10-12 hours | Serves: 8-10

Ingredients:
- Beef brisket
- Coffee grounds
- Brown sugar
- Paprika
- Garlic powder
- Onion powder
- Salt and pepper

Instructions:
1. Mix coffee grounds, brown sugar, paprika, garlic powder, onion powder, salt, and pepper for the rub.
2. Rub brisket with the coffee rub and let marinate overnight.
3. Smoke on Traeger grill at 225°F until tender.
4. Rest before slicing thinly for a flavorful brisket experience.

Beef and Asparagus Roll-Ups

Prep Time: 20 minutes | Cooking Time: 10 minutes | Serves: 4

Ingredients:
- Thinly sliced beef sirloin or flank steak
- Asparagus spears, trimmed
- Olive oil
- Salt and pepper to taste
- Cream cheese
- Garlic powder

- Fresh basil leaves

Instructions:
1. Marinate beef slices in olive oil, salt, and pepper.
2. Grill asparagus spears until slightly charred.
3. Spread cream cheese on beef slices, sprinkle with garlic powder.
4. Place a grilled asparagus spear and basil leaf on each slice.
5. Roll up and secure with toothpicks.
6. Grill roll-ups until beef is cooked to your liking.

Pork Belly Tacos
Prep Time: 20 minutes | Cooking Time: 3 hours | Serves: 4

Ingredients:
- Pork belly strips
- Taco seasoning
- Corn or flour tortillas
- Avocado slices
- Cilantro, chopped
- Lime wedges

Instructions:
1. Rub pork belly strips with taco seasoning.
2. Smoke on Traeger grill at 250°F until crispy and tender.
3. Slice or chop smoked pork belly.
4. Warm tortillas on the grill.
5. Fill tortillas with pork belly, avocado slices, cilantro, and a squeeze of lime.

Beef and Pineapple Skewers with Teriyaki Glaze
Prep Time: 30 minutes | Cooking Time: 15 minutes | Serves: 4

Ingredients:
- Beef sirloin or tenderloin, cubed
- Pineapple chunks
- Teriyaki sauce
- Soy sauce
- Brown sugar
- Garlic, minced
- Sesame seeds for garnish

Instructions:
1. Marinate beef cubes in teriyaki sauce, soy sauce,

brown sugar, and minced garlic.
2. Thread beef and pineapple onto skewers.
3. Grill on Traeger until beef is cooked and pineapple is caramelized.
4. Brush with extra teriyaki sauce before serving.
5. Sprinkle with sesame seeds for garnish.

Pork Tenderloin with Mustard Glaze
Prep Time: 15 minutes | Cooking Time: 1 hour | Serves: 4-6

Ingredients:
- Pork tenderloin
- Olive oil
- Salt and pepper to taste
- Dijon mustard
- Honey
- Apple cider vinegar
- Fresh thyme, chopped

Instructions:
1. Rub pork tenderloin with olive oil, salt, and pepper.
2. Smoke on Traeger grill at 275°F until internal temperature reaches 145°F.
3. Mix Dijon mustard, honey, apple cider vinegar, and chopped thyme for glaze.
4. Brush glaze on smoked pork tenderloin during the last 15 minutes of cooking.
5. Let rest before slicing and serving.

Beef Stuffed Portobello Mushrooms
Prep Time: 20 minutes | Cooking Time: 15 minutes | Serves: 4

Ingredients:
- Portobello mushrooms, stems removed
- Ground beef
- Onion, diced
- Garlic, minced
- Spinach leaves
- Mozzarella cheese, shredded
- Italian seasoning

Instructions:
1. In a skillet, cook ground beef with diced onion and minced garlic.
2. Season with Italian seasoning.
3. Fill portobello mushrooms with cooked beef mixture, spinach leaves, and shredded mozzarella.

4. Grill stuffed mushrooms on Traeger until cheese is melted and mushrooms are tender.
5. Serve hot as a flavorful and satisfying dish.

Pork Loin Roast with Herb Crust

Prep Time: 15 minutes | Cooking Time: 1.5 hours | Serves: 6-8

Ingredients:
• Pork loin roast
• Olive oil
• Salt and pepper to taste
• Dijon mustard
• Fresh herbs (rosemary, thyme, sage), chopped
• Breadcrumbs

Instructions:
1. Rub pork loin roast with olive oil, salt, and pepper.
2. Spread Dijon mustard over the top and sides of the roast.
3. Mix chopped fresh herbs with breadcrumbs to make the herb crust.
4. Press herb crust onto the mustard-coated pork loin.
5. Smoke on Traeger grill at 275°F until internal temperature reaches 145°F.
6. Let rest before slicing and serving.

Beef and Black Bean Quesadillas

Prep Time: 20 minutes | Cooking Time: 10 minutes | Serves: 4

Ingredients:
• Thinly sliced beef
• Black beans, drained and rinsed
• Shredded cheese (cheddar, Monterey Jack)
• Flour tortillas
• Cilantro, chopped
• Sour cream, salsa

Instructions:
1. Grill thinly sliced beef on Traeger until cooked.
2. Heat flour tortillas on the grill.
3. Spread black beans, cooked beef, shredded cheese, and chopped cilantro on one half of each tortilla.
4. Fold tortillas in half to create quesadillas.
5. Grill quesadillas until cheese is melted and tortillas are crispy.
6. Serve hot with sour cream and salsa.

Pork Spare Ribs

Prep Time: 20 minutes | Cooking Time: 5 hours | Serves: 4-6

Ingredients:
• Pork spare ribs
• BBQ rub
• Apple cider vinegar
• Ketchup
• Brown sugar
• Worcestershire sauce
• Garlic powder
• Onion powder
• Paprika

Instructions:
1. Rub pork spare ribs with BBQ rub and let them marinate.
2. Smoke on Traeger grill at 225°F until tender and juicy.
3. Mix apple cider vinegar, ketchup, brown sugar, Worcestershire sauce, garlic powder, onion powder, and paprika for homemade BBQ sauce.
4. Brush ribs with BBQ sauce during the last hour of smoking.
5. Serve smoked pork spare ribs with extra BBQ sauce on the side.

Beef and Veggie Wraps with Avocado Sauce

Prep Time: 30 minutes | Cooking Time: 15 minutes | Serves: 4

Ingredients:
• Thinly sliced beef (sirloin or flank steak)
• Bell peppers, sliced
• Onion, sliced
• Zucchini, sliced
• Tortillas
• Avocado, mashed
• Lime juice
• Cumin
• Fresh cilantro, chopped

Instructions:
1. Marinate beef slices in olive oil, cumin, salt, and pepper.
2. Grill beef and veggies on Traeger until cooked and slightly charred.

3. Mix mashed avocado with lime juice and chopped cilantro for avocado sauce.
4. Spread avocado sauce on tortillas, top with grilled beef and veggies.
5. Roll up the wraps and serve as a flavorful meal.

Pork Loin Chops with Maple Mustard Glaze

Prep Time: 15 minutes | **Cooking Time:** 1 hour | **Serves:** 4

Ingredients:
- Pork loin chops
- Olive oil
- Salt and pepper to taste
- Maple syrup
- Dijon mustard
- Apple cider vinegar
- Garlic powder

Instructions:
1. Rub pork loin chops with olive oil, salt, and pepper.
2. Smoke on Traeger grill at 275°F until internal temperature reaches 145°F.
3. Mix maple syrup, Dijon mustard, apple cider vinegar, and garlic powder for glaze.
4. Brush glaze on smoked pork loin chops during the last 15 minutes of cooking.
5. Let rest before serving with extra glaze on the side.

Lamb Chops with Mint Chimichurri

Prep Time: 20 minutes | **Cooking Time:** 10 minutes | **Serves:** 4

Ingredients:
- Lamb chops
- Olive oil
- Salt and pepper to taste
- Fresh mint leaves, chopped
- Fresh parsley, chopped
- Garlic, minced
- Red wine vinegar
- Lemon juice
- Red pepper flakes

Instructions:
1. Rub lamb chops with olive oil, salt, and pepper.
2. Marinate for at least 30 minutes.
3. Preheat Traeger grill to high heat.
4. Grill lamb chops for 3-4 minutes per side for medium-rare.

5. In a blender, combine chopped mint, parsley, garlic, red wine vinegar, lemon juice, and red pepper flakes.
6. Blend until smooth to make mint chimichurri sauce.
7. Serve grilled lamb chops with mint chimichurri on top.

Leg of Lamb with Rosemary Garlic Rub

Prep Time: 30 minutes | **Cooking Time:** 2 hours | **Serves:** 6-8

Ingredients:
- Leg of lamb, bone-in
- Olive oil
- Salt and pepper to taste
- Fresh rosemary, chopped
- Garlic cloves, minced
- Lemon zest
- Dijon mustard

Instructions:
1. Make a rub with olive oil, salt, pepper, chopped rosemary, minced garlic, lemon zest, and Dijon mustard.
2. Rub the mixture all over the leg of lamb.
3. Marinate in the refrigerator for at least 4 hours or overnight.
4. Preheat Traeger grill to 275°F.
5. Smoke the leg of lamb for about 2 hours or until the internal temperature reaches 135°F for medium-rare.
6. Rest the lamb for 15 minutes before slicing and serving.

Lamb Kebabs with Yogurt Marinade

Prep Time: 30 minutes | **Cooking Time:** 10 minutes | **Serves:** 4

Ingredients:
- Lamb shoulder or leg, cubed
- Plain yogurt
- Lemon juice
- Garlic, minced
- Paprika
- Cumin
- Salt and pepper to taste
- Red onion, cut into chunks
- Bell peppers, cut into chunks

Instructions:
1. In a bowl, mix yogurt, lemon juice, minced garlic,

paprika, cumin, salt, and pepper.
2. Add cubed lamb to the marinade, coat well, and refrigerate for at least 2 hours.
3. Preheat Traeger grill to medium-high heat.
4. Thread marinated lamb, red onion, and bell peppers onto skewers.
5. Grill lamb kebabs for about 10 minutes, turning occasionally, until lamb is cooked and veggies are tender.
6. Serve hot with a side of couscous or rice.

Lamb Ribs with Spicy BBQ Glaze
Prep Time: 20 minutes | Cooking Time: 4 hours | Serves: 4-6

Ingredients:
- Lamb ribs
- BBQ rub
- Apple cider vinegar
- Tomato paste
- Brown sugar
- Worcestershire sauce
- Hot sauce (adjust to taste)
- Garlic powder
- Onion powder

Instructions:
1. Rub lamb ribs with BBQ rub and let them marinate.
2. Preheat Traeger grill to 225°F.
3. Smoke lamb ribs for about 3 hours.
4. In a saucepan, combine apple cider vinegar, tomato paste, brown sugar, Worcestershire sauce, hot sauce, garlic powder, and onion powder for the glaze.
5. Brush glaze on smoked lamb ribs and continue smoking for another hour.
6. Serve hot with extra glaze on the side.

Lamb Burgers with Feta and Tzatziki Sauce
Prep Time: 30 minutes | Cooking Time: 10 minutes | Serves: 4
Ingredients:
- Ground lamb
- Red onion, finely chopped
- Fresh parsley, chopped
- Feta cheese, crumbled
- Salt and pepper to taste
- Burger buns
- Tzatziki sauce

- Lettuce, tomato, cucumber

Instructions:
1. In a bowl, mix ground lamb, chopped red onion, chopped parsley, crumbled feta, salt, and pepper.
2. Form the mixture into burger patties.
3. Preheat Traeger grill to medium-high heat.
4. Grill lamb burgers for about 4-5 minutes per side or until desired doneness.
5. Toast burger buns on the grill.
6. Assemble burgers with lettuce, tomato, cucumber, and a generous dollop of tzatziki sauce.

Lamb Shoulder with Herb Rub
Prep Time: 30 minutes | Cooking Time: 6 hours | Serves: 6-8

Ingredients:
- Lamb shoulder, bone-in
- Olive oil
- Salt and pepper to taste
- Fresh thyme, rosemary, and oregano, chopped
- Garlic cloves, minced
- Lemon juice

Instructions:
1. Rub lamb shoulder with olive oil, salt, and pepper.
2. Combine chopped herbs, minced garlic, and lemon juice to make the herb rub.
3. Rub the herb mixture all over the lamb shoulder.
4. Marinate in the refrigerator for at least 4 hours or overnight.
5. Preheat Traeger grill to 225°F.
6. Smoke lamb shoulder for about 6 hours or until tender and falling off the bone.
7. Rest before carving and serving.

Lamb Meatballs with Tomato Sauce
Prep Time: 30 minutes | Cooking Time: 20 minutes | Serves: 4

Ingredients:
- Ground lamb
- Bread crumbs
- Egg
- Onion, finely chopped
- Garlic, minced
- Fresh mint, chopped
- Salt and pepper to taste

- Olive oil
- Tomato sauce
- Parmesan cheese, grated

Instructions:

1. In a bowl, mix ground lamb, bread crumbs, egg, chopped onion, minced garlic, chopped mint, salt, and pepper.
2. Form the mixture into meatballs.
3. Preheat Traeger grill to medium heat.
4. Grill lamb meatballs for about 10 minutes, turning occasionally, until cooked through.
5. Heat tomato sauce in a pan on the grill.
6. Serve grilled lamb meatballs with tomato sauce and grated Parmesan cheese.

Lamb Shoulder Chops with Garlic Herb Butter

Prep Time: 20 minutes | Cooking Time: 1 hour | Serves: 4

Ingredients:
- Lamb shoulder chops
- Olive oil
- Salt and pepper to taste
- Fresh thyme and rosemary, chopped
- Garlic cloves, minced
- Butter, softened

Instructions:

1. Rub lamb shoulder chops with olive oil, salt, and pepper.
2. Combine chopped herbs, minced garlic, and softened butter to make the herb butter.
3. Spread herb butter on both sides of the lamb chops.
4. Marinate in the refrigerator for at least 30 minutes.
5. Preheat Traeger grill to medium-high heat.
6. Smoke lamb shoulder chops for about 1 hour or until cooked to your liking.
7. Serve hot with extra herb butter on top.

Lamb Gyros with Tzatziki Sauce

Prep Time: 30 minutes | Cooking Time: 10 minutes | Serves: 4

Ingredients:
- Lamb leg or shoulder, thinly sliced
- Olive oil
- Lemon juice
- Garlic, minced

- Dried oregano
- Salt and pepper to taste
- Pita bread
- Tzatziki sauce
- Sliced tomatoes, onions, and cucumbers

Instructions:

1. In a bowl, mix sliced lamb with olive oil, lemon juice, minced garlic, dried oregano, salt, and pepper.
2. Marinate for at least 2 hours.
3. Preheat Traeger grill to medium-high heat.
4. Grill marinated lamb slices for about 2-3 minutes per side until cooked through.
5. Warm pita bread on the grill.
6. Assemble gyros with grilled lamb, tzatziki sauce, and sliced vegetables.
7. Wrap and serve immediately.

Lamb Shanks with Red Wine Sauce

Prep Time: 30 minutes | Cooking Time: 4 hours | Serves: 4

Ingredients:
- Lamb shanks
- Olive oil
- Salt and pepper to taste
- Red wine
- Beef broth
- Onion, chopped
- Carrots, chopped
- Celery, chopped
- Fresh rosemary and thyme

Instructions:

1. Rub lamb shanks with olive oil, salt, and pepper.
2. Marinate in red wine and fresh herbs for at least 4 hours or overnight.
3. Preheat Traeger grill to 275°F.
4. Smoke lamb shanks for about 3 hours.
5. In a Dutch oven or foil pan, combine lamb shanks, chopped onion, carrots, celery, beef broth, and more red wine.
6. Cover and continue smoking for another hour or until lamb is tender.
7. Serve lamb shanks with the flavorful red wine sauce.

Chapter 8: Fish and Seafood

Salmon with Lemon Herb Butter

Prep Time: 15 minutes | Cooking Time: 15 minutes | Serves: 4

Ingredients:
- Salmon fillets
- Olive oil
- Salt and pepper to taste
- Fresh dill, chopped
- Lemon slices
- Butter, softened

Instructions:
1. Rub salmon fillets with olive oil, salt, pepper, and chopped dill.
2. Preheat Traeger grill to medium-high heat.
3. Grill salmon fillets skin-side down for about 6-8 minutes.
4. Flip carefully and continue grilling for another 6-8 minutes until cooked through.
5. Meanwhile, mix softened butter with chopped dill and a squeeze of lemon juice for herb butter.
6. Serve grilled salmon with a dollop of lemon herb butter on top.

Shrimp Skewers with Garlic Butter

Prep Time: 20 minutes | Cooking Time: 10 minutes | Serves: 4

Ingredients:
- Large shrimp, peeled and deveined
- Olive oil
- Salt and pepper to taste
- Garlic cloves, minced
- Butter, melted
- Fresh parsley, chopped

Instructions:
1. Marinate shrimp in olive oil, salt, pepper, and minced garlic for at least 30 minutes.
2. Preheat Traeger grill to medium heat.
3. Thread shrimp onto skewers.
4. Grill shrimp skewers for about 3-4 minutes per side until pink and cooked.
5. Meanwhile, mix melted butter with chopped parsley and a pinch of garlic.
6. Brush garlic butter over grilled shrimp skewers before serving.

Swordfish Steaks with Mediterranean Salsa

Prep Time: 20 minutes | Cooking Time: 10 minutes | Serves: 4

Ingredients:
- Swordfish steaks
- Olive oil
- Salt and pepper to taste
- Lemon zest
- Cherry tomatoes, halved
- Kalamata olives, chopped
- Red onion, finely chopped
- Fresh basil, chopped
- Balsamic vinegar

Instructions:
1. Rub swordfish steaks with olive oil, salt, pepper, and lemon zest.
2. Marinate for at least 30 minutes.
3. Preheat Traeger grill to medium-high heat.
4. Grill swordfish steaks for about 4-5 minutes per side until grill marks appear and fish is cooked through.
5. Meanwhile, mix halved cherry tomatoes, chopped olives, finely chopped red onion, chopped basil, and a drizzle of balsamic vinegar for the salsa.
6. Serve grilled swordfish steaks with Mediterranean salsa on top.

Lobster Tails with Garlic Herb Butter

Prep Time: 20 minutes | Cooking Time: 20 minutes | Serves: 2

Ingredients:
- Lobster tails, split lengthwise
- Olive oil
- Salt and pepper to taste
- Garlic cloves, minced
- Butter, softened
- Fresh parsley, chopped

Instructions:
1. Brush lobster tails with olive oil and season with salt and pepper.
2. Preheat Traeger grill to medium heat.
3. Place lobster tails flesh-side down on the grill.
4. Smoke lobster tails for about 15-20 minutes until meat is opaque and cooked through.
5. Meanwhile, mix minced garlic, softened butter, and

chopped parsley for garlic herb butter.
6. Serve smoked lobster tails with a generous dollop of garlic herb butter.

Halibut with Mango Salsa
Prep Time: 20 minutes | Cooking Time: 10 minutes | Serves: 4

Ingredients:
- Halibut fillets
- Olive oil
- Salt and pepper to taste
- Lime zest
- Fresh cilantro, chopped
- Mango, diced
- Red bell pepper, diced
- Red onion, finely chopped
- Jalapeno, seeded and minced
- Lime juice

Instructions:
1. Rub halibut fillets with olive oil, salt, pepper, lime zest, and chopped cilantro.
2. Marinate for at least 30 minutes.
3. Preheat Traeger grill to medium-high heat.
4. Grill halibut fillets for about 4-5 minutes per side until fish flakes easily with a fork.
5. Meanwhile, mix diced mango, diced red bell pepper, finely chopped red onion, minced jalapeno, lime juice, and chopped cilantro for mango salsa.
6. Serve grilled halibut with mango salsa spooned over the top.

Cedar Plank Salmon
Prep Time: 15 minutes | Cooking Time: 15 minutes | Serves: 4

Ingredients:
- Salmon fillets
- Cedar plank (soaked in water)
- Olive oil
- Salt and pepper to taste
- Lemon slices
- Fresh dill, for garnish

Instructions:
1. Preheat Traeger grill to medium-high heat.
2. Brush soaked cedar plank with olive oil and place salmon fillets on top.

3. Season salmon with salt, pepper, and lemon slices on top.
4. Grill cedar plank salmon for about 12-15 minutes until fish is cooked through and cedar plank is lightly charred.
5. Garnish with fresh dill before serving.

Scallops with Bacon Wrapped Asparagus
Prep Time: 20 minutes | Cooking Time: 15 minutes | Serves: 4

Ingredients:
- Fresh scallops
- Asparagus spears
- Bacon slices
- Olive oil
- Salt and pepper to taste
- Lemon wedges, for serving

Instructions:
1. Preheat Traeger grill to medium heat.
2. Wrap each scallop with a piece of bacon and secure with a toothpick.
3. Toss asparagus spears with olive oil, salt, and pepper.
4. Grill bacon-wrapped scallops and asparagus spears for about 7-8 minutes, turning occasionally, until bacon is crispy and scallops are cooked.
5. Serve smoked scallops and bacon-wrapped asparagus with lemon wedges.

Shrimp Tacos with Pineapple Salsa
Prep Time: 30 minutes | Cooking Time: 10 minutes | Serves: 4

Ingredients:
- Large shrimp, peeled and deveined
- Olive oil
- Taco seasoning
- Corn or flour tortillas
- Pineapple, diced
- Red onion, finely chopped
- Fresh cilantro, chopped
- Jalapeno, minced
- Lime juice
- Avocado slices, for serving

Instructions:
1. Toss shrimp with olive oil and taco seasoning.
2. Preheat Traeger grill to medium-high heat.

3. Grill shrimp for about 2-3 minutes per side until pink and cooked.
4. In a bowl, mix diced pineapple, chopped red onion, chopped cilantro, minced jalapeno, and lime juice for pineapple salsa.
5. Warm tortillas on the grill.
6. Assemble shrimp tacos with pineapple salsa and avocado slices.

Crab Legs with Garlic Butter

Prep Time: 10 minutes | Cooking Time: 20 minutes | Serves: 4

Ingredients:
- Crab legs, thawed if frozen
- Olive oil
- Salt and pepper to taste
- Old Bay seasoning
- Garlic butter

Instructions:
1. Brush crab legs with olive oil and season with salt, pepper, and Old Bay seasoning if desired.
2. Preheat Traeger grill to medium heat.
3. Place crab legs on the grill and smoke for about 15-20 minutes until heated through.
4. Serve smoked crab legs with garlic butter for dipping.

Lobster Tails with Herb Citrus Butter

Prep Time: 20 minutes | Cooking Time: 10 minutes | Serves: 2

Ingredients:
- Lobster tails, split lengthwise
- Olive oil
- Salt and pepper to taste
- Fresh parsley, chopped
- Fresh thyme, chopped
- Lemon zest
- Butter, softened

Instructions:
1. Brush lobster tails with olive oil and season with salt and pepper.
2. Preheat Traeger grill to medium-high heat.
3. Grill lobster tails flesh-side down for about 5 minutes.
4. Flip carefully and continue grilling for another 5

minutes until meat is opaque and cooked through.
5. Meanwhile, mix chopped parsley, chopped thyme, lemon zest, and softened butter for herb citrus butter.
6. Serve grilled lobster tails with herb citrus butter on the side.

Mahi Mahi with Mango Salsa

Prep Time: 20 minutes | Cooking Time: 10 minutes | Serves: 4

Ingredients:
- Mahi Mahi fillets
- Olive oil
- Salt and pepper to taste
- Lime juice
- Fresh cilantro, chopped
- Mango, diced
- Red bell pepper, diced
- Red onion, finely chopped
- Jalapeno, minced

Instructions:
1. Rub Mahi Mahi fillets with olive oil, salt, pepper, and lime juice.
2. Marinate for at least 30 minutes.
3. Preheat Traeger grill to medium-high heat.
4. Grill Mahi Mahi fillets for about 4-5 minutes per side until fish flakes easily with a fork.
5. Meanwhile, mix diced mango, diced red bell pepper, finely chopped red onion, minced jalapeno, lime juice, and chopped cilantro for mango salsa.
6. Serve grilled Mahi Mahi with mango salsa on top.

Trout with Herb Butter

Prep Time: 15 minutes | Cooking Time: 20 minutes | Serves: 4

Ingredients:
- Whole trout, cleaned and gutted
- Olive oil
- Salt and pepper to taste
- Fresh thyme and rosemary, chopped
- Lemon slices
- Butter, softened

Instructions:
1. Rub trout with olive oil, salt, pepper, and chopped herbs.
2. Marinate for at least 30 minutes.

3. Preheat Traeger grill to medium heat.
4. Stuff trout cavity with lemon slices and a spoonful of softened butter.
5. Place trout on the grill and smoke for about 15-20 minutes until fish is cooked and flaky.
6. Serve smoked trout with herb butter on the side.

Swordfish Tacos with Chipotle Crema
Prep Time: 30 minutes | Cooking Time: 10 minutes | Serves: 4

Ingredients:
- Swordfish steaks
- Olive oil
- Salt and pepper to taste
- Corn or flour tortillas
- Cabbage slaw (shredded cabbage, carrots, cilantro, lime juice)
- Chipotle peppers in adobo sauce
- Sour cream
- Lime wedges, for serving

Instructions:
1. Rub swordfish steaks with olive oil, salt, and pepper.
2. Marinate for at least 30 minutes.
3. Preheat Traeger grill to medium-high heat.
4. Grill swordfish steaks for about 3-4 minutes per side until cooked.
5. Meanwhile, blend chipotle peppers in adobo sauce with sour cream to make chipotle crema.
6. Warm tortillas on the grill.
7. Assemble swordfish tacos with cabbage slaw, chipotle crema, and lime wedges.

Crab Cakes with Remoulade Sauce
Prep Time: 30 minutes | Cooking Time: 20 minutes | Serves: 4

Ingredients:
- Lump crab meat
- Bread crumbs
- Mayonnaise
- Dijon mustard
- Old Bay seasoning
- Green onions, chopped
- Egg
- Olive oil
- Remoulade sauce

Instructions:
1. In a bowl, mix lump crab meat, bread crumbs, mayonnaise, Dijon mustard, Old Bay seasoning, chopped green onions, and egg.
2. Form the mixture into crab cakes.
3. Preheat Traeger grill to medium heat.
4. Brush crab cakes with olive oil and grill for about 8-10 minutes per side until golden and cooked.
5. Serve smoked crab cakes with remoulade sauce on the side.

Halibut Steaks with Herb Butter
Prep Time: 20 minutes | Cooking Time: 10 minutes | Serves: 4

Ingredients:
- Halibut steaks
- Olive oil
- Salt and pepper to taste
- Fresh parsley and dill, chopped
- Lemon juice
- Butter, softened

Instructions:
1. Rub halibut steaks with olive oil, salt, pepper, chopped parsley, chopped dill, and lemon juice.
2. Marinate for at least 30 minutes.
3. Preheat Traeger grill to medium-high heat.
4. Grill halibut steaks for about 4-5 minutes per side until fish flakes easily with a fork.
5. Meanwhile, mix softened butter with chopped parsley and dill to make herb butter.
6. Serve grilled halibut steaks with a dollop of herb butter on top.

Stuffed Squid with Chorizo and Rice
Prep Time: 30 minutes | Cooking Time: 30 minutes | Serves: 4

Ingredients:
- Squid tubes, cleaned and tentacles reserved
- Chorizo sausage, casing removed
- Cooked rice
- Onion, finely chopped
- Garlic, minced
- Tomato paste
- Paprika
- Salt and pepper to taste
- Olive oil

- Lemon wedges, for serving

Instructions:

1. In a skillet, sauté chorizo, chopped onion, minced garlic, tomato paste, paprika, salt, and pepper until cooked.
2. Mix cooked rice with chorizo mixture.
3. Stuff squid tubes with the chorizo and rice stuffing.
4. Preheat Traeger grill to medium heat.
5. Grill stuffed squid tubes and reserved tentacles for about 15 minutes, turning occasionally, until squid is cooked and filling is heated through.
6. Serve smoked stuffed squid with lemon wedges on the side.

Tuna Steaks with Sesame Soy Glaze

Prep Time: 15 minutes | Cooking Time: 10 minutes | Serves: 4

Ingredients:
- Tuna steaks
- Soy sauce
- Rice vinegar
- Sesame oil
- Honey
- Garlic, minced
- Fresh ginger, grated
- Sesame seeds, for garnish
- Green onions, chopped

Instructions:

1. In a bowl, whisk together soy sauce, rice vinegar, sesame oil, honey, minced garlic, and grated ginger to make the marinade.
2. Marinate tuna steaks in the mixture for at least 30 minutes.
3. Preheat Traeger grill to medium-high heat.
4. Grill tuna steaks for about 2-3 minutes per side until desired doneness.
5. Meanwhile, simmer the marinade in a saucepan until slightly thickened to make the glaze.
6. Brush grilled tuna steaks with sesame soy glaze and garnish with sesame seeds and chopped green onions.

Mussels with White Wine and Garlic

Prep Time: 15 minutes | Cooking Time: 15 minutes | Serves: 4

Ingredients:
- Fresh mussels, cleaned and debearded
- Olive oil
- Garlic, minced
- White wine
- Butter
- Fresh parsley, chopped
- Lemon wedges, for serving

Instructions:

1. In a large skillet, heat olive oil and sauté minced garlic until fragrant.
2. Add cleaned mussels and white wine to the skillet.
3. Cover and cook for about 10-12 minutes until mussels open.
4. Stir in butter and chopped parsley until melted and combined.
5. Preheat Traeger grill to medium heat.
6. Transfer cooked mussels to a grill-safe pan and smoke for about 5 minutes.
7. Serve smoked mussels with garlic white wine sauce and lemon wedges.

Lobster Rolls

Prep Time: 30 minutes | Cooking Time: 10 minutes | Serves: 4

Ingredients:
- Lobster meat, cooked and chopped
- Celery, finely chopped
- Mayonnaise
- Lemon juice
- Fresh dill, chopped
- Salt and pepper to taste
- Butter
- Hot dog buns or rolls

Instructions:

1. In a bowl, mix chopped lobster meat, finely chopped celery, mayonnaise, lemon juice, chopped dill, salt, and pepper.
2. Butter hot dog buns or rolls on the inside.
3. Preheat Traeger grill to medium heat.
4. Grill buttered buns or rolls until lightly toasted.
5. Fill toasted buns with lobster salad mixture.

6. Serve Traeger grilled lobster rolls immediately.

Smoked Salmon Dip
Prep Time: 15 minutes | Cooking Time: 30 minutes | Serves: 6-8

Ingredients:
- Smoked salmon, flaked
- Cream cheese, softened
- Sour cream
- Lemon juice
- Dill, chopped
- Green onions, chopped
- Salt and pepper to taste
- Crackers or sliced baguette, for serving

Instructions:
1. In a bowl, mix flaked smoked salmon, softened cream cheese, sour cream, lemon juice, chopped dill, chopped green onions, salt, and pepper.
2. Preheat Traeger grill to low heat for smoking.
3. Transfer salmon dip mixture to a grill-safe dish.
4. Place the dish on the grill and smoke for about 30 minutes until flavors meld and dip is lightly infused with smoke.
5. Serve Traeger smoked salmon dip with crackers or sliced baguette.

Lemon Garlic Butter Shrimp Skewers
Prep Time: 20 minutes | Cooking Time: 8 minutes | Serves: 4

Ingredients:
- Large shrimp, peeled and deveined
- Olive oil
- Lemon zest
- Garlic, minced
- Butter, melted
- Fresh parsley, chopped
- Salt and pepper to taste

Instructions:
1. In a bowl, mix olive oil, lemon zest, minced garlic, melted butter, chopped parsley, salt, and pepper.
2. Marinate shrimp in the mixture for 15 minutes.
3. Preheat Traeger grill to medium-high heat.
4. Thread shrimp onto skewers.
5. Grill shrimp skewers for about 3-4 minutes per side until pink and cooked through.

6. Serve grilled shrimp skewers with lemon wedges.

Bacon-Wrapped Scallops
Prep Time: 15 minutes | Cooking Time: 15 minutes | Serves: 4

Ingredients:
- Large scallops
- Bacon slices
- Olive oil
- Salt and pepper to taste
- Toothpicks

Instructions:
1. Season scallops with salt and pepper.
2. Wrap each scallop with a slice of bacon and secure with a toothpick.
3. Preheat Traeger grill to medium heat.
4. Grill bacon-wrapped scallops for about 6-7 minutes per side until bacon is crispy and scallops are cooked.
5. Serve smoked bacon-wrapped scallops as appetizers or with a side dish.

Tuna Nicoise Salad
Prep Time: 30 minutes | Cooking Time: 10 minutes | Serves: 4

Ingredients:
- Ahi tuna steaks
- Olive oil
- Salt and pepper to taste
- Mixed greens
- Cherry tomatoes, halved
- Hard-boiled eggs, sliced
- Kalamata olives
- Red onion, thinly sliced
- Green beans, blanched
- Anchovy fillets (optional)
- Balsamic vinaigrette

Instructions:
1. Rub tuna steaks with olive oil, salt, and pepper.
2. Preheat Traeger grill to high heat.
3. Grill tuna steaks for about 2-3 minutes per side until seared on the outside but still rare inside.
4. Assemble mixed greens, cherry tomatoes, hard-boiled eggs, Kalamata olives, sliced red onion, and blanched green beans on a platter.
5. Top with grilled tuna steaks and anchovy fillets if

using.

6. Drizzle with balsamic vinaigrette before serving.

Lobster Mac and Cheese

Prep Time: 30 minutes | Cooking Time: 1 hour | Serves: 6-8

Ingredients:
- Lobster meat, cooked and chopped
- Elbow macaroni, cooked
- Butter
- Flour
- Milk
- Cheddar cheese, grated
- Parmesan cheese, grated
- Bread crumbs
- Salt and pepper to taste

Instructions:

1. Preheat Traeger grill to 350°F (175°C) for smoking.
2. In a saucepan, melt butter and whisk in flour to make a roux.
3. Gradually add milk while whisking until smooth and thickened.
4. Stir in grated cheddar cheese and grated Parmesan cheese until melted and creamy.
5. Mix cooked elbow macaroni and chopped lobster meat into the cheese sauce.
6. Transfer the mac and cheese mixture to a greased baking dish.
7. Top with bread crumbs and additional grated cheese.
8. Smoke on the Traeger grill for about 30-40 minutes until bubbly and golden.
9. Let it rest for a few minutes before serving.

Grilled Stuffed Calamari

Prep Time: 30 minutes | Cooking Time: 15 minutes | Serves: 4

Ingredients:
- Calamari tubes, cleaned
- Cooked quinoa or rice
- Cherry tomatoes, diced
- Fresh basil, chopped
- Garlic, minced
- Olive oil
- Lemon juice
- Salt and pepper to taste
- Toothpicks

Instructions:

1. In a bowl, mix cooked quinoa or rice, diced cherry tomatoes, chopped basil, minced garlic, olive oil, lemon juice, salt, and pepper.
2. Stuff calamari tubes with the quinoa or rice mixture.
3. Secure the ends with toothpicks to keep the stuffing in place.
4. Preheat Traeger grill to medium-high heat.
5. Grill stuffed calamari tubes for about 6-8 minutes per side until cooked and slightly charred.
6. Serve Traeger grilled stuffed calamari as a flavorful appetizer or main dish.

Crab-Stuffed Mushrooms

Prep Time: 20 minutes | Cooking Time: 20 minutes | Serves: 4

Ingredients:
- Large mushrooms, cleaned and stems removed
- Lump crab meat
- Cream cheese
- Parmesan cheese, grated
- Green onions, chopped
- Garlic powder
- Salt and pepper to taste
- Bread crumbs

Instructions:

1. In a bowl, mix lump crab meat, cream cheese, grated Parmesan cheese, chopped green onions, garlic powder, salt, and pepper.
2. Stuff mushroom caps with the crab mixture.
3. Sprinkle bread crumbs on top of stuffed mushrooms.
4. Preheat Traeger grill to 375°F (190°C) for smoking.
5. Place stuffed mushrooms on a grill-safe pan and smoke for about 15-20 minutes until mushrooms are tender and filling is heated through.
6. Serve Traeger smoked crab-stuffed mushrooms as a savory appetizer.

Grilled Snapper Veracruz

Prep Time: 30 minutes | Cooking Time: 20 minutes | Serves: 4

Ingredients:
- Red snapper fillets
- Olive oil
- Salt and pepper to taste
- Onion, thinly sliced
- Garlic, minced
- Bell peppers (red and green), sliced
- Cherry tomatoes, halved
- Olives, sliced
- Capers
- Jalapeno, sliced (optional for heat)
- White wine
- Fresh cilantro, chopped

Instructions:
1. Rub snapper fillets with olive oil, salt, and pepper.
2. Preheat Traeger grill to medium-high heat.
3. Grill snapper fillets for about 4-5 minutes per side until fish is cooked through.
4. In a skillet, sauté onion, minced garlic, sliced bell peppers, cherry tomatoes, olives, capers, and jalapeno until softened.
5. Add white wine to the skillet and simmer until reduced slightly.
6. Stir in chopped cilantro.
7. Serve grilled snapper fillets topped with Veracruz sauce.

Smoked Oysters Rockefeller

Prep Time: 15 minutes | Cooking Time: 15 minutes | Serves: 4

Ingredients:
- Fresh oysters, shucked
- Spinach, chopped
- Bacon, cooked and crumbled
- Parmesan cheese, grated
- Bread crumbs
- Butter
- Garlic, minced
- Lemon wedges, for serving

Instructions:
1. Preheat Traeger grill to 375°F (190°C) for smoking.
2. In a skillet, sauté chopped spinach with minced garlic until wilted.
3. Remove skillet from heat and mix in crumbled bacon, grated Parmesan cheese, and bread crumbs.
4. Place shucked oysters on a grill-safe pan.
5. Top each oyster with the spinach mixture and a small piece of butter.
6. Smoke oysters on the Traeger grill for about 10-15 minutes until topping is golden and bubbly.
7. Serve Traeger smoked oysters Rockefeller with lemon wedges.

Octopus with Chimichurri Sauce

Prep Time: 30 minutes | Cooking Time: 20 minutes | Serves: 4

Ingredients:
- Octopus, cleaned and tentacles separated
- Olive oil
- Salt and pepper to taste
- Chimichurri sauce (parsley, cilantro, garlic, red wine vinegar, olive oil)

Instructions:
1. Marinate octopus tentacles in olive oil, salt, and pepper for at least 1 hour.
2. Preheat Traeger grill to medium-high heat.
3. Grill octopus tentacles for about 10 minutes per side until charred and tender.
4. Meanwhile, prepare chimichurri sauce by blending parsley, cilantro, minced garlic, red wine vinegar, and olive oil until smooth.
5. Serve grilled octopus with chimichurri sauce drizzled on top.

Chapter 9: Vegetarian Dishes

Grilled Portobello Mushroom Burgers

Prep Time: 10 minutes | Cooking Time: 10 minutes | Serves: 4

Ingredients:
- Portobello mushroom caps
- Olive oil
- Balsamic vinegar
- Salt and pepper to taste
- Burger buns
- Lettuce, tomato slices, onion slices (for toppings)
- Avocado slices (optional)
- Burger sauce (mayonnaise, ketchup, mustard)

Instructions:
1. Brush Portobello mushroom caps with olive oil and balsamic vinegar.
2. Season with salt and pepper.
3. Preheat Traeger grill to medium-high heat.
4. Grill mushroom caps for about 4-5 minutes per side until tender.
5. Toast burger buns on the grill.
6. Assemble burgers with grilled mushroom caps, lettuce, tomato, onion, avocado slices, and burger sauce.

Grilled Vegetable Skewers

Prep Time: 15 minutes | Cooking Time: 10-12 minutes | Serves: 4

Ingredients:
- Assorted vegetables (bell peppers, zucchini, cherry tomatoes, onions, mushrooms, etc.)
- Olive oil
- Garlic powder, onion powder, Italian seasoning
- Salt and pepper to taste

Instructions:
1. Cut vegetables into chunks or slices.
2. Thread vegetables onto skewers.
3. Brush with olive oil and sprinkle with garlic powder, onion powder, Italian seasoning, salt, and pepper.
4. Preheat Traeger grill to medium heat.
5. Grill vegetable skewers for about 10-12 minutes, turning occasionally, until tender and lightly charred.
6. Serve Traeger grilled vegetable skewers as a side dish or main course.

Smoked Stuffed Bell Peppers

Prep Time: 20 minutes | Cooking Time: 30-35 minutes | Serves: 4

Ingredients:
- Bell peppers, halved and seeds removed
- Cooked quinoa or rice
- Black beans, drained and rinsed
- Corn kernels
- Diced tomatoes
- Onion, finely chopped
- Garlic, minced
- Mexican seasoning blend
- Shredded cheese
- Fresh cilantro, chopped

Instructions:
1. In a bowl, mix cooked quinoa or rice, black beans, corn kernels, diced tomatoes, chopped onion, minced garlic, and Mexican seasoning.
2. Stuff bell pepper halves with the quinoa or rice mixture.
3. Preheat Traeger grill to medium heat.
4. Place stuffed bell peppers on a grill-safe pan.
5. Smoke on the Traeger grill for about 25-30 minutes until peppers are tender and filling is heated through.
6. Sprinkle shredded cheese on top and continue smoking for another 5 minutes until cheese melts.
7. Garnish with chopped cilantro before serving.

Grilled Eggplant Parmesan

Prep Time: 15 minutes | Cooking Time: 25-30 minutes | Serves: 4

Ingredients:
- Eggplant, sliced into rounds
- Olive oil
- Italian breadcrumbs
- Marinara sauce
- Mozzarella cheese, grated
- Parmesan cheese, grated
- Fresh basil leaves
- Salt and pepper to taste

Instructions:
1. Brush eggplant slices with olive oil and coat with Italian breadcrumbs.
2. Preheat Traeger grill to medium-high heat.
3. Grill eggplant slices for about 3-4 minutes per side

until golden and tender.

4. In a baking dish, layer grilled eggplant slices with marinara sauce, grated mozzarella cheese, and grated Parmesan cheese.

5. Repeat layers and top with fresh basil leaves.

6. Cover the dish with foil and place it on the grill.

7. Smoke for about 20-25 minutes until cheese is melted and bubbly.

8. Serve Traeger grilled eggplant Parmesan hot.

Butternut Squash Soup

Prep Time: 15 minutes | Cooking Time: 50-60 minutes | Serves: 6

Ingredients:
• Butternut squash, peeled, seeded, and cubed
• Onion, chopped
• Carrots, chopped
• Celery, chopped
• Vegetable broth
• Coconut milk
• Curry powder
• Salt and pepper to taste
• Fresh cilantro, chopped

Instructions:
1. In a large pot, sauté chopped onion, carrots, and celery until softened.
2. Add cubed butternut squash, vegetable broth, coconut milk, curry powder, salt, and pepper.
3. Bring to a boil, then reduce heat and simmer until squash is tender.
4. Using an immersion blender or regular blender, puree the soup until smooth.
5. Preheat Traeger grill to low heat for smoking.
6. Transfer the pureed soup to a grill-safe pot or pan.
7. Smoke on the Traeger grill for about 20-30 minutes to infuse smoky flavor.
8. Garnish with chopped cilantro before serving.

Grilled Cauliflower Steaks

Prep Time: 10 minutes | Cooking Time: 12 minutes | Serves: 4

Ingredients:
• Cauliflower, sliced into thick steaks
• Olive oil
• Garlic powder, paprika, cumin
• Lemon juice

• Salt and pepper to taste
• Fresh parsley, chopped

Instructions:
1. Brush cauliflower steaks with olive oil and season with garlic powder, paprika, cumin, lemon juice, salt, and pepper.
2. Preheat Traeger grill to medium-high heat.
3. Grill cauliflower steaks for about 5-6 minutes per side until tender and grill marks appear.
4. Transfer grilled cauliflower steaks to a serving platter.
5. Garnish with chopped fresh parsley before serving.

Smoked Vegetable Lasagna

Prep Time: 30 minutes | Cooking Time: 30 minutes | Serves: 6-8

Ingredients:
• Lasagna noodles, cooked
• Marinara sauce
• Assorted grilled vegetables
• Ricotta cheese
• Mozzarella cheese, grated
• Parmesan cheese, grated
• Fresh basil leaves
• Salt and pepper to taste

Instructions:
1. Preheat Traeger grill to 375°F (190°C) for smoking.
2. In a baking dish, spread a layer of marinara sauce.
3. Layer cooked lasagna noodles, grilled vegetables, ricotta cheese, grated mozzarella cheese, and grated Parmesan cheese.
4. Repeat layers until the dish is filled, ending with a layer of sauce and cheese on top.
5. Cover the dish with foil and place it on the grill.
6. Smoke for about 25-30 minutes until lasagna is bubbly and cheese is melted.
7. Garnish with fresh basil leaves before serving.

Grilled Stuffed Acorn Squash

Prep Time: 20 minutes | Cooking Time: 25 minutes | Serves: 4

Ingredients:
• Acorn squash, halved and seeds removed
• Olive oil
• Quinoa or rice, cooked
• Chickpeas, drained and rinsed
• Dried cranberries

- Pecans, chopped
- Maple syrup
- Cinnamon
- Salt and pepper to taste

Instructions:
1. Brush acorn squash halves with olive oil and season with salt and pepper.
2. In a bowl, mix cooked quinoa or rice, chickpeas, dried cranberries, chopped pecans, maple syrup, and cinnamon.
3. Stuff acorn squash halves with the quinoa or rice mixture.
4. Preheat Traeger grill to medium heat.
5. Grill stuffed acorn squash for about 20-25 minutes until squash is tender and filling is heated through.
6. Serve Traeger grilled stuffed acorn squash as a wholesome meal.

Spinach and Ricotta Stuffed Portobello Mushrooms
Prep Time: 15 minutes | Cooking Time: 20 minutes | Serves: 4

Ingredients:
- Portobello mushroom caps
- Olive oil
- Baby spinach
- Ricotta cheese
- Parmesan cheese, grated
- Garlic, minced
- Nutmeg
- Salt and pepper to taste

Instructions:
1. Brush Portobello mushroom caps with olive oil and season with salt and pepper.
2. Preheat Traeger grill to medium-high heat.
3. Grill mushroom caps for about 4-5 minutes per side until tender.
4. In a skillet, sauté baby spinach with minced garlic until wilted.
5. In a bowl, mix sautéed spinach with ricotta cheese, grated Parmesan cheese, nutmeg, salt, and pepper.
6. Stuff mushroom caps with the spinach and ricotta mixture.
7. Return stuffed mushrooms to the grill and smoke for another 10 minutes until filling is warmed through.
8. Serve Traeger smoked spinach and ricotta stuffed

Portobello mushrooms as a flavorful appetizer or main dish.

Sweet Potato Tacos
Prep Time: 15 minutes | Cooking Time: 15 minutes | Serves: 4

Ingredients:
- Sweet potatoes, peeled and diced
- Olive oil
- Smoked paprika, cumin, garlic powder
- Black beans, drained and rinsed
- Corn tortillas
- Avocado slices
- Lime wedges
- Fresh cilantro, chopped
- Salsa or hot sauce

Instructions:
1. Toss diced sweet potatoes with olive oil, smoked paprika, cumin, garlic powder, salt, and pepper.
2. Preheat Traeger grill to medium-high heat.
3. Grill sweet potatoes in a grill basket or on skewers until tender and slightly charred.
4. Warm corn tortillas on the grill.
5. Fill tortillas with grilled sweet potatoes, black beans, avocado slices, chopped cilantro, and a squeeze of lime juice.
6. Serve Traeger grilled sweet potato tacos with salsa or hot sauce if desired.

Caprese Stuffed Portobello Mushrooms
Prep Time: 10 minutes | Cooking Time: 15 minutes | Serves: 4

Ingredients:
- Portobello mushroom caps
- Fresh mozzarella cheese, sliced
- Cherry tomatoes, halved
- Fresh basil leaves
- Balsamic glaze
- Olive oil
- Salt and pepper to taste

Instructions:
1. Brush mushroom caps with olive oil and season with salt and pepper.
2. Preheat Traeger grill to medium heat.
3. Grill mushroom caps for about 5 minutes per side

until tender.

4. Fill mushroom caps with sliced mozzarella, cherry tomato halves, and fresh basil leaves.

5. Return stuffed mushrooms to the grill and smoke for another 5 minutes until cheese melts.

6. Drizzle with balsamic glaze before serving.

Eggplant and Chickpea Curry

Prep Time: 15 minutes | Cooking Time: 45 minutes | Serves: 4

Ingredients:
- Eggplant, diced
- Chickpeas, cooked
- Onion, chopped
- Garlic, minced
- Ginger, grated
- Curry powder
- Coconut milk
- Tomato sauce
- Fresh cilantro, chopped
- Salt and pepper to taste

Instructions:

1. In a skillet, sauté chopped onion, minced garlic, and grated ginger until fragrant.

2. Add diced eggplant and cook until softened.

3. Stir in cooked chickpeas, curry powder, coconut milk, tomato sauce, salt, and pepper.

4. Simmer for 10-15 minutes until flavors blend and sauce thickens.

5. Preheat Traeger grill to low heat for smoking.

6. Transfer the curry mixture to a grill-safe pot or pan.

7. Smoke on the Traeger grill for about 20-30 minutes to enhance the smoky flavor.

8. Garnish with chopped cilantro before serving with rice or naan.

Quinoa-Stuffed Bell Peppers

Prep Time: 20 minutes | Cooking Time: 30-35 minutes | Serves: 4

Ingredients:
- Bell peppers, halved and seeds removed
- Cooked quinoa
- Black beans, drained and rinsed
- Corn kernels
- Diced tomatoes
- Onion, finely chopped
- Garlic, minced
- Mexican seasoning blend
- Shredded cheese
- Fresh cilantro, chopped

Instructions:

1. In a bowl, mix cooked quinoa, black beans, corn kernels, diced tomatoes, chopped onion, minced garlic, and Mexican seasoning.

2. Stuff bell pepper halves with the quinoa mixture.

3. Preheat Traeger grill to medium heat.

4. Place stuffed bell peppers on a grill-safe pan.

5. Smoke on the Traeger grill for about 25-30 minutes until peppers are tender and filling is heated through.

6. Sprinkle shredded cheese on top and continue smoking for another 5 minutes until cheese melts.

7. Garnish with chopped cilantro before serving.

Greek Stuffed Portobello Mushrooms

Prep Time: 15 minutes | Cooking Time: 15 minutes | Serves: 4

Ingredients:
- Portobello mushroom caps
- Feta cheese, crumbled
- Spinach, chopped
- Kalamata olives, chopped
- Red onion, finely chopped
- Garlic, minced
- Olive oil
- Lemon juice
- Dried oregano
- Salt and pepper to taste

Instructions:

1. Brush mushroom caps with olive oil and season with salt, pepper, and dried oregano.

2. Preheat Traeger grill to medium-high heat.

3. Grill mushroom caps for about 5 minutes per side until softened.

4. In a skillet, sauté chopped spinach, minced garlic, chopped olives, and red onion until wilted.

5. Fill mushroom caps with the spinach mixture and crumbled feta cheese.

6. Return stuffed mushrooms to the grill and smoke for another 5 minutes until cheese is melted.

7. Drizzle with lemon juice before serving.

Sweet Potato and Black Bean Enchiladas

Prep Time: 20 minutes | Cooking Time: 45-50 minutes | Serves: 4

Ingredients:
- Sweet potatoes, peeled and diced
- Black beans, cooked
- Onion, chopped
- Garlic, minced
- Enchilada sauce
- Tortillas (corn or flour)
- Shredded cheese
- Fresh cilantro, chopped
- Avocado slices
- Lime wedges
- Salt and pepper to taste

Instructions:
1. Preheat Traeger grill to 375°F (190°C) for smoking.
2. Toss diced sweet potatoes with olive oil, salt, and pepper.
3. Spread sweet potatoes on a grill-safe pan and smoke for about 20-25 minutes until tender.
4. In a skillet, sauté chopped onion and minced garlic until translucent.
5. Add cooked black beans to the skillet and heat through.
6. Fill tortillas with smoked sweet potatoes, black bean mixture, and shredded cheese.
7. Roll up the tortillas and place them in a baking dish.
8. Pour enchilada sauce over the rolled tortillas and sprinkle with additional cheese.
9. Smoke the enchiladas on the Traeger grill for about 15-20 minutes until cheese is melted and bubbly.
10. Garnish with chopped cilantro and serve with avocado slices and lime wedges.

Stuffed Bell Peppers with Quinoa

Prep Time: 20 minutes | Cooking Time: 30 minutes | Serves: 4

Ingredients:
- Bell peppers, halved and seeds removed
- Cooked quinoa
- Cooked lentils
- Onion, chopped
- Garlic, minced
- Tomato sauce
- Italian seasoning
- Shredded mozzarella cheese
- Fresh parsley, chopped
- Salt and pepper to taste

Instructions:
1. Preheat Traeger grill to medium heat.
2. In a skillet, sauté chopped onion and minced garlic until softened.
3. Add cooked quinoa, cooked lentils, tomato sauce, Italian seasoning, salt, and pepper to the skillet.
4. Simmer for 5-10 minutes until flavors meld.
5. Fill bell pepper halves with the quinoa-lentil mixture.
6. Place stuffed peppers on a grill-safe pan and sprinkle shredded mozzarella cheese on top.
7. Grill on the Traeger for about 15-20 minutes until peppers are tender and cheese is melted.
8. Garnish with chopped parsley before serving.

Vegetable Paella

Prep Time: 20 minutes | Cooking Time: 45 minutes | Serves: 4-6

Ingredients:
- Arborio rice
- Vegetable broth
- Onion, chopped
- Bell peppers, diced
- Zucchini, diced
- Cherry tomatoes, halved
- Artichoke hearts, quartered
- Green peas
- Spanish saffron threads
- Paprika
- Olive oil
- Lemon wedges
- Fresh parsley, chopped
- Salt and pepper to taste

Instructions:
1. Preheat Traeger grill to medium heat.
2. In a large paella pan or skillet, sauté chopped onion until translucent.
3. Add diced bell peppers, zucchini, cherry tomatoes, artichoke hearts, and green peas to the pan.
4. Stir in Arborio rice, Spanish saffron threads, paprika, salt, and pepper.
5. Pour vegetable broth over the rice and vegetables, covering everything evenly.

6. Cover the paella pan with foil and place it on the grill.
7. Smoke for about 25-30 minutes until rice is cooked and absorbs the flavors.
8. Garnish with fresh parsley and serve with lemon wedges.

Portobello Mushroom Steaks

Prep Time: 15 minutes | Cooking Time: 12 minutes | Serves: 4

Ingredients:
- Portobello mushroom caps
- Olive oil
- Balsamic vinegar
- Garlic powder, onion powder, smoked paprika
- Salt and pepper to taste
- Fresh parsley, chopped
- Fresh cilantro, chopped
- Fresh oregano, chopped
- Red wine vinegar
- Red pepper flakes

Instructions:
1. Brush mushroom caps with olive oil and balsamic vinegar.
2. Season with garlic powder, onion powder, smoked paprika, salt, and pepper.
3. Preheat Traeger grill to medium-high heat.
4. Grill mushroom caps for about 5-6 minutes per side until tender.
5. In a bowl, mix chopped parsley, cilantro, oregano, minced garlic, red wine vinegar, salt, pepper, and red pepper flakes.
6. Drizzle chimichurri sauce over grilled mushroom steaks before serving.

Stuffed Acorn Squash with Wild Rice

Prep Time: 20 minutes | Cooking Time: 30 minutes | Serves: 4

Ingredients:
- Acorn squash, halved and seeds removed
- Cooked wild rice
- Dried cranberries
- Pecans, chopped
- Maple syrup
- Cinnamon
- Salt and pepper to taste

Instructions:
1. Preheat Traeger grill to 375°F (190°C) for smoking.
2. In a bowl, mix cooked wild rice, dried cranberries, chopped pecans, maple syrup, cinnamon, salt, and pepper.
3. Stuff acorn squash halves with the wild rice mixture.
4. Place stuffed acorn squash on a grill-safe pan.
5. Smoke on the Traeger grill for about 25-30 minutes until squash is tender and filling is heated through.
6. Serve smoked stuffed acorn squash as a delightful vegetarian dish.

Chapter 10: Desserts

Grilled Pineapple with Coconut Whipped Cream

Prep Time: 10 minutes | Cooking Time: 6 minutes | Serves: 4

Ingredients:
- Pineapple slices
- Brown sugar
- Coconut milk
- Vanilla extract
- Honey
- Shredded coconut

Instructions:
1. Sprinkle pineapple slices with brown sugar.
2. Preheat Traeger grill to medium-high heat.
3. Grill pineapple slices for about 2-3 minutes per side until caramelized.
4. In a chilled bowl, whip coconut milk with vanilla extract and honey until fluffy.
5. Serve grilled pineapple with a dollop of coconut whipped cream.
6. Garnish with toasted shredded coconut.

Chocolate Banana S'mores

Prep Time: 5 minutes | Cooking Time: 10 minutes | Serves: 4

Ingredients:
- Ripe bananas, halved lengthwise
- Chocolate chips or chunks
- Mini marshmallows
- Graham crackers

Instructions:
1. Place banana halves on a grill-safe pan.
2. Fill banana halves with chocolate chips or chunks and mini marshmallows.
3. Preheat Traeger grill to medium heat.
4. Smoke bananas for about 10 minutes until chocolate melts and marshmallows are toasted.
5. Serve smoked banana s'mores with graham crackers for dipping.

Strawberry Shortcake Skewers

Prep Time: 10 minutes | Cooking Time: 6 minutes | Serves: 4

Ingredients:
- Fresh strawberries, hulled
- Pound cake or angel food cake, cubed
- Wooden skewers
- Whipped cream
- Fresh mint leaves

Instructions:
1. Thread strawberries and cake cubes onto wooden skewers.
2. Preheat Traeger grill to medium-high heat.
3. Grill skewers for about 2-3 minutes per side until lightly charred.
4. Serve grilled strawberry shortcake skewers with a dollop of whipped cream.
5. Garnish with fresh mint leaves.

Smoked Peach Crisp

Prep Time: 15 minutes | Cooking Time: 20-25 minutes | Serves: 6

Ingredients:
- Fresh peaches, sliced
- Brown sugar
- Cinnamon
- Rolled oats
- Flour
- Butter, cold and cubed
- Vanilla ice cream

Instructions:
1. Toss sliced peaches with brown sugar and cinnamon.
2. In a bowl, mix rolled oats, flour, and cold cubed butter to make the crisp topping.
3. Preheat Traeger grill to medium heat.
4. Place peaches in a grill-safe baking dish and sprinkle the crisp topping over them.
5. Smoke the peach crisp for about 20-25 minutes until topping is golden and peaches are tender.
6. Serve smoked peach crisp warm, optionally with a scoop of vanilla ice cream.

Watermelon with Mint and Feta

Prep Time: 10 minutes | Cooking Time: 4 minutes | Serves: 4

Ingredients:
- Watermelon slices
- Olive oil
- Fresh mint leaves, chopped
- Feta cheese, crumbled
- Balsamic glaze
- Sea salt

Instructions:
1. Brush watermelon slices with olive oil.
2. Preheat Traeger grill to medium-high heat.
3. Grill watermelon slices for about 2 minutes per side until grill marks appear.
4. Arrange grilled watermelon on a serving platter.
5. Sprinkle with chopped mint, crumbled feta cheese, and a drizzle of balsamic glaze.
6. Finish with a sprinkle of sea salt before serving.

Smoked Apple Crisp

Prep Time: 15 minutes | Cooking Time: 20-25 minutes | Serves: 6

Ingredients:
- Apples, peeled and sliced
- Lemon juice
- Brown sugar
- Cinnamon
- Rolled oats
- Flour
- Butter, cold and cubed
- Vanilla extract

Instructions:
1. Toss sliced apples with lemon juice, brown sugar, and cinnamon.
2. In a bowl, mix rolled oats, flour, cold cubed butter, and vanilla extract to make the crisp topping.
3. Preheat Traeger grill to medium heat.
4. Place apples in a grill-safe baking dish and sprinkle the crisp topping over them.
5. Smoke the apple crisp for about 20-25 minutes until topping is golden and apples are tender.
6. Serve smoked apple crisp warm, optionally with a scoop of vanilla ice cream.

Banana Split Foil Packets

Prep Time: 10 minutes | Cooking Time: 10-12 minutes | Serves: 4

Ingredients:
- Ripe bananas, halved lengthwise
- Chocolate chips
- Mini marshmallows
- Chopped walnuts
- Maraschino cherries
- Vanilla ice cream
- Aluminum foil

Instructions:
1. Place each banana half on a piece of aluminum foil.
2. Fill banana halves with chocolate chips, mini marshmallows, chopped nuts, and a cherry.
3. Wrap the foil tightly around each banana split packet.
4. Preheat Traeger grill to medium heat.
5. Grill foil packets for about 10-12 minutes until chocolate melts and bananas are soft.
6. Carefully open the foil packets and serve banana splits with a scoop of vanilla ice cream.

Chocolate Chip Cookies

Prep Time: 15 minutes | Cooking Time: 10-12 minutes | Serves: 24 cookies

Ingredients:
- All-purpose flour
- Baking soda
- Salt
- Butter, softened
- Brown sugar
- Granulated sugar
- Eggs
- Vanilla extract
- Chocolate chips

Instructions:
1. In a bowl, whisk together flour, baking soda, and salt.
2. In another bowl, cream together softened butter, brown sugar, and granulated sugar.
3. Beat in eggs and vanilla extract until well combined.
4. Gradually add the flour mixture to the wet ingredients, mixing until dough forms.
5. Fold in chocolate chips.

6. Preheat Traeger grill to 350°F (175°C) for smoking.
7. Drop cookie dough by spoonfuls onto a grill-safe baking sheet.
8. Smoke cookies on the Traeger grill for about 10-12 minutes until golden around the edges.
9. Let cookies cool slightly before serving.

Fruit Salad with Honey-Lime Dressing

Prep Time: 15 minutes | Cooking Time: 6 minutes | Serves: 4-6

Ingredients:
- Assorted fruits (pineapple, strawberries, peaches, and grapes)
- Honey
- Lime juice
- Fresh mint leaves, chopped
- Greek yogurt

Instructions:
1. Toss sliced fruits with honey, lime juice, and chopped mint in a bowl.
2. Preheat Traeger grill to medium-high heat.
3. Grill fruit slices for about 2-3 minutes per side until lightly caramelized.
4. Arrange grilled fruit on a serving platter.
5. Drizzle with any remaining honey-lime dressing.
6. Serve grilled fruit salad with a dollop of Greek yogurt if desired.

Nutella-Stuffed French Toast

Prep Time: 15 minutes | Cooking Time: 8 minutes | Serves: 4

Ingredients:
- Sliced brioche or challah bread
- Nutella or chocolate hazelnut spread
- Eggs
- Milk
- Vanilla extract
- Ground cinnamon
- Butter
- Powdered sugar (for dusting)
- Fresh berries (for garnish)

Instructions:
1. Spread Nutella or chocolate hazelnut spread between two slices of bread to make sandwiches.
2. In a bowl, whisk together eggs, milk, vanilla extract, and ground cinnamon to make the French toast batter.
3. Dip each sandwich in the batter, coating both sides.
4. Preheat Traeger grill to medium heat.
5. Melt butter on a griddle or grill pan.
6. Grill stuffed French toast sandwiches for about 3-4 minutes per side until golden and cooked through.
7. Dust with powdered sugar and garnish with fresh berries before serving.

Grilled Peach Cobbler

Prep Time: 20 minutes | Cooking Time: 30-35 minutes | Serves: 6-8

Ingredients:
- Fresh peaches, sliced
- Granulated sugar
- Lemon juice
- Cornstarch
- Ground cinnamon
- All-purpose flour
- Baking powder
- Salt
- Unsalted butter, cold and cubed
- Milk
- Vanilla extract

Instructions:
1. Toss sliced peaches with granulated sugar, lemon juice, cornstarch, and ground cinnamon.
2. Preheat Traeger grill to 375°F (190°C).
3. In a mixing bowl, combine flour, baking powder, salt, and additional sugar.
4. Cut in cold cubed butter until the mixture resembles coarse crumbs.
5. Stir in milk and vanilla extract to form a dough.
6. Spread the peach mixture in a baking dish and drop spoonfuls of dough over the top.
7. Place the baking dish on the grill and bake for about 30-35 minutes until the topping is golden brown and the filling is bubbly.
8. Serve warm with a scoop of vanilla ice cream.

Smoked Banana Bread

Prep Time: 15 minutes | Cooking Time: 50-60 minutes | Serves: 8-10

Ingredients:
- Ripe bananas, mashed
- Granulated sugar
- Vegetable oil
- Eggs
- Vanilla extract
- All-purpose flour
- Baking soda
- Salt
- Cinnamon

Instructions:
1. Preheat Traeger grill to 350°F (175°C) for smoking.
2. In a mixing bowl, combine mashed bananas, granulated sugar, vegetable oil, eggs, and vanilla extract.
3. In a separate bowl, whisk together flour, baking soda, salt, and cinnamon.
4. Gradually add the dry ingredients to the wet ingredients, mixing until just combined.
5. Fold in chopped nuts if desired.
6. Pour the batter into a greased loaf pan.
7. Place the loaf pan on the grill and smoke for about 50-60 minutes until a toothpick inserted into the center comes out clean.
8. Let the banana bread cool before slicing and serving.

Pound Cake with Berries and Whipped Cream

Prep Time: 15 minutes | Cooking Time: 4 minutes | Serves: 4

Ingredients:
- Store-bought or homemade pound cake, sliced
- Fresh berries
- Granulated sugar
- Lemon juice
- Heavy cream
- Powdered sugar
- Vanilla extract

Instructions:
1. Toss fresh berries with granulated sugar and lemon juice in a bowl. Let them macerate for about 15-20 minutes.
2. Preheat Traeger grill to medium-high heat.
3. Grill pound cake slices for about 1-2 minutes per side until lightly toasted.
4. In a separate bowl, whip heavy cream with powdered sugar and vanilla extract until soft peaks form.
5. Arrange grilled pound cake slices on serving plates.
6. Top with macerated berries and a dollop of whipped cream.
7. Serve immediately as a delightful dessert.

Chocolate Covered Strawberries

Prep Time: 10 minutes | Cooking Time: 20-30 minutes | Serves: 4

Ingredients:
- Fresh strawberries, washed and dried
- Dark chocolate chips or melting chocolate
- White chocolate chips
- Coconut oil

Instructions:
1. Preheat Traeger grill to 200°F (93°C) for smoking.
2. Line a baking sheet with parchment paper.
3. In separate microwave-safe bowls, melt dark chocolate chips and white chocolate chips (if using) with a teaspoon of coconut oil for smoother consistency.
4. Dip each strawberry into the melted chocolate, coating about two-thirds of the berry.
5. Place the chocolate-covered strawberries on the prepared baking sheet.
6. Transfer the baking sheet to the grill and smoke for about 20-30 minutes until the chocolate sets.
7. Remove from the grill and let them cool before serving.

Grilled Lemon Bars

Prep Time: 20 minutes | Cooking Time: 35-45 minutes | Serves: 12

Ingredients:
- Unsalted butter, softened
- Granulated sugar
- All-purpose flour
- Salt
- Eggs
- Fresh lemon juice
- Lemon zest

- Powdered sugar

Instructions:
1. Preheat Traeger grill to 350°F (175°C) for smoking.
2. In a mixing bowl, cream together softened butter and granulated sugar.
3. Gradually add flour and salt, mixing until crumbly.
4. Press the mixture into the bottom of a greased baking dish to form the crust.
5. Bake the crust on the grill for about 15-20 minutes until lightly golden.
6. In another bowl, whisk together eggs, fresh lemon juice, and lemon zest until well combined.
7. Pour the lemon mixture over the baked crust and return to the grill.
8. Smoke for an additional 20-25 minutes until the filling is set.
9. Let the lemon bars cool before dusting with powdered sugar and slicing.

Smoked Pecan Pie

Prep Time: 15 minutes | Cooking Time: 45-50 minutes | Serves: 8

Ingredients:
- Pie crust
- Eggs
- Granulated sugar
- Dark corn syrup
- Butter, melted
- Vanilla extract
- Salt
- Pecan halves

Instructions:
1. Preheat Traeger grill to 375°F (190°C) for smoking.
2. Line a pie dish with the pie crust and crimp the edges.
3. In a mixing bowl, beat eggs, granulated sugar, dark corn syrup, melted butter, vanilla extract, and salt until well combined.
4. Stir in pecan halves until evenly distributed.
5. Pour the pecan filling into the prepared pie crust.
6. Place the pie on the grill and smoke for about 45-50 minutes until the filling is set and the crust is golden brown.
7. Remove from the grill and let the pie cool completely before slicing and serving.

Pineapple Upside-Down Cake

Prep Time: 20 minutes | Cooking Time: 30-35 minutes | Serves: 8-10

Ingredients:
- Fresh pineapple slices
- Brown sugar
- Maraschino cherries
- Unsalted butter, melted
- All-purpose flour
- Granulated sugar
- Baking powder
- Salt
- Eggs
- Vanilla extract
- Milk

Instructions:
1. Preheat Traeger grill to 350°F (175°C) for smoking.
2. Grease a round cake pan and arrange pineapple slices in the bottom.
3. Place a maraschino cherry in the center of each pineapple slice.
4. Sprinkle brown sugar over the pineapple slices.
5. In a mixing bowl, beat melted butter, granulated sugar, eggs, and vanilla extract until creamy.
6. Gradually add flour, baking powder, salt, and milk, mixing until smooth.
7. Pour the batter over the pineapple slices in the cake pan.
8. Place the cake pan on the grill and smoke for about 30-35 minutes until a toothpick inserted into the center comes out clean.
9. Let the cake cool for a few minutes before inverting onto a serving plate.

Almond Butter Cookies

Prep Time: 15 minutes | Cooking Time: 10-12 minutes | Serves: 24 cookies

Ingredients:
- Almond butter
- Granulated sugar
- Brown sugar
- Eggs
- Vanilla extract
- Baking soda
- Salt
- Sliced almonds

Instructions:
1. Preheat Traeger grill to 350°F (175°C) for smoking.
2. In a mixing bowl, cream together almond butter, granulated sugar, brown sugar, eggs, and vanilla extract until smooth.
3. Add baking soda and salt, mixing until combined.
4. Roll the cookie dough into balls and place them on a greased baking sheet.
5. Flatten each cookie slightly with a fork and press a few sliced almonds on top if desired.
6. Smoke the cookies on the grill for about 10-12 minutes until edges are golden.
7. Let the cookies cool on the baking sheet before transferring to a wire rack.

Apple Crisp Bars

Prep Time: 20 minutes | Cooking Time: 35-40 minutes | Serves: 12

Ingredients:
- Apples, peeled and diced
- Lemon juice
- Granulated sugar
- Cornstarch
- Ground cinnamon
- Rolled oats
- All-purpose flour
- Brown sugar
- Unsalted butter, melted
- Salt

Instructions:
1. Preheat Traeger grill to 375°F (190°C) for smoking.
2. Toss diced apples with lemon juice, granulated sugar, cornstarch, and ground cinnamon in a bowl.
3. In another bowl, mix rolled oats, flour, brown sugar, melted butter, and salt to make the crumble topping.
4. Press half of the crumble mixture into the bottom of a greased baking dish.
5. Spread the apple mixture over the crust layer.
6. Sprinkle the remaining crumble mixture over the apples.
7. Place the baking dish on the grill and smoke for about 35-40 minutes until golden and bubbly.
8. Let the apple crisp bars cool before slicing into squares.

Bourbon Pecan Pie Bars

Prep Time: 15 minutes | Cooking Time: 30-35 minutes | Serves: 12

Ingredients:
- Shortbread crust (store-bought or homemade)
- Pecan halves
- Eggs
- Granulated sugar
- Dark corn syrup
- Bourbon
- Vanilla extract
- Salt

Instructions:
1. Preheat Traeger grill to 350°F (175°C) for smoking.
2. Place pecan halves evenly over the shortbread crust in a baking dish.
3. In a mixing bowl, beat eggs, granulated sugar, dark corn syrup, bourbon, vanilla extract, and salt until well combined.
4. Pour the bourbon-pecan mixture over the pecans and crust.
5. Place the baking dish on the grill and smoke for about 30-35 minutes until the filling is set.
6. Let the pie bars cool completely before slicing into bars.

Beef Brisket

Prep Time: 30 minutes | Cooking Time: 10-15 hours | Serves: 10-12

Ingredients:
- Beef brisket
- Beef rub or seasoning blend
- Wood pellets

Instructions:
1. Season the beef brisket generously with your favorite beef rub or seasoning blend, covering all sides.
2. Preheat your Traeger grill to 225°F (107°C) using hickory or oak wood pellets for smoking.
3. Place the seasoned brisket on the grill grates and close the lid.
4. Smoke the brisket for about 1 hour per pound, or until the internal temperature reaches 195-205°F (90-96°C) for tender slices.
5. Remove the brisket from the grill and let it rest for 30 minutes before slicing against the grain and serving.

Smoked Pork Shoulder (Pulled Pork)

Prep Time: 20 minutes | Cooking Time: 10-14 hours | Serves: 8-10

Ingredients:
- Pork shoulder (bone-in or boneless)
- Pork rub or seasoning blend
- Applewood pellets

Instructions:
1. Rub the pork shoulder with your preferred pork rub or seasoning blend, covering it thoroughly.
2. Preheat your Traeger grill to 225°F (107°C) using applewood pellets for a sweet, smoky flavor.
3. Place the seasoned pork shoulder on the grill and close the lid.
4. Smoke the pork shoulder for about 1.5 hours per pound, or until the internal temperature reaches 195-205°F (90-96°C) for easy shredding.
5. Let the pork shoulder rest for 30-60 minutes, then shred the meat using two forks.
6. Serve the pulled pork with your favorite barbecue sauce and sides.

Smoked Whole Chicken

Prep Time: 15 minutes | Cooking Time: 3-4 hours | Serves: 4-6

Ingredients:
- Whole chicken
- Chicken rub or seasoning blend
- Poultry pellets

Instructions:
1. Season the whole chicken inside and out with your chosen chicken rub or seasoning blend.
2. Preheat your Traeger grill to 250°F (121°C) using apple or cherry wood pellets for a mild, fruity smoke flavor.
3. Place the seasoned chicken directly on the grill grates, breast side up.
4. Smoke the chicken for approximately 3-4 hours or until the internal temperature in the thickest part of the thigh reaches 165°F (74°C) for safe consumption.
5. Remove the smoked chicken from the grill and let it rest for 10-15 minutes before carving and serving.

Traeger Smoked Salmon

Prep Time: 10 minutes | Cooking Time: 1-2 hours | Serves: 4-6

Ingredients:
- Salmon fillets or sides
- Seafood rub or seasoning blend
- Alderwood pellets

Instructions:
1. Pat the salmon fillets or sides dry with paper towels.
2. Season the salmon generously with your preferred seafood rub or seasoning blend.
3. Preheat your Traeger grill to 180°F (82°C) using alderwood pellets for a delicate, smoky flavor that complements seafood.
4. Place the seasoned salmon directly on the grill grates, skin side down.
5. Smoke the salmon for about 1-2 hours, depending on the thickness, until it reaches an internal temperature of 145°F (63°C) for moist, flaky fish.
6. Remove the smoked salmon from the grill and serve hot or cold with lemon wedges.

Smoked Vegetarian Chili

Prep Time: 20 minutes | Cooking Time: 4-6 hours | Serves: 6-8

Ingredients:
- Assorted beans
- Diced tomatoes
- Onion, diced
- Bell peppers, diced
- Corn kernels
- Vegetable broth
- Chili seasoning mix or spices
- Wood-fired salsa
- Wood pellets of choice

Instructions:
1. In a large cast-iron Dutch oven or grill-safe pot, combine the assorted beans, diced tomatoes, diced onion, diced bell peppers, corn kernels, vegetable broth, chili seasoning mix or spices, and wood-fired salsa if using.
2. Preheat your Traeger grill to 225°F (107°C) using your preferred wood pellets for smoking.
3. Place the Dutch oven or pot on the grill and close the lid.
4. Smoke the vegetarian chili for about 4-6 hours, stirring occasionally, until the flavors meld and the beans are tender.
5. Adjust seasoning if needed and serve the smoked vegetarian chili hot with toppings like shredded cheese, sour cream, and chopped cilantro.

Smoked Beef Ribs

Prep Time: 15 minutes | Cooking Time: 5-6 hours | Serves: 4-6

Ingredients:
- Beef back ribs
- Beef rub or seasoning blend
- Wood pellets

Instructions:
1. Rub the beef ribs with your favorite beef rub or seasoning blend, covering all sides.
2. Preheat your Traeger grill to 225°F (107°C) using mesquite or oak wood pellets for a robust smoke flavor.
3. Place the seasoned beef ribs on the grill grates and close the lid.
4. Smoke the beef ribs for about 5-6 hours, or until the

meat is tender and easily pulls away from the bone.
5. Remove the smoked beef ribs from the grill and let them rest for 10-15 minutes before slicing and serving.

Smoked Stuffed Peppers

Prep Time: 20 minutes | Cooking Time: 2-3 hours | Serves: 4

Ingredients:
- Bell peppers (any color), halved and seeded
- Ground beef or turkey
- Onion, finely chopped
- Garlic, minced
- Cooked rice
- Tomato sauce
- Shredded cheese (cheddar or mozzarella)
- Italian seasoning
- Salt and pepper
- Wood pellets of choice

Instructions:
1. In a skillet, cook ground beef or turkey with chopped onion, minced garlic, and Italian seasoning until browned.
2. Stir in cooked rice and tomato sauce, and season with salt and pepper.
3. Preheat your Traeger grill to 250°F (121°C) using applewood or hickory pellets for smoking.
4. Fill halved bell peppers with the meat and rice mixture, then top with shredded cheese.
5. Place the stuffed peppers on the grill and smoke for about 2-3 hours until the peppers are tender and the cheese is melted and bubbly.
6. Remove from the grill and let them cool slightly before serving.

Smoked Pork Belly Burnt Ends

Prep Time: 15 minutes | Cooking Time: 3.5-4.5 hours | Serves: 6-8

Ingredients:
- Pork belly, cubed
- Pork rub or seasoning blend
- Barbecue sauce
- Wood pellets

Instructions:
1. Season the cubed pork belly with your preferred pork rub or seasoning blend.

2. Preheat your Traeger grill to 250°F (121°C) using maple or pecan wood pellets for a sweet, nutty smoke flavor.

3. Place the seasoned pork belly cubes in a disposable aluminum pan or grill-safe pan.

4. Smoke the pork belly cubes for about 3-4 hours, or until they develop a caramelized crust.

5. Remove the pan from the grill and toss the pork belly cubes in barbecue sauce.

6. Return the pan to the grill and smoke for an additional 30 minutes to let the sauce caramelize.

7. Remove from the grill and serve the pork belly burnt ends as a flavorful appetizer or main dish.

Smoked Texas Turkey Breast

Prep Time: 15 minutes | Cooking Time: 3-4 hours | Serves: 6-8

Ingredients:
- Turkey breast (bone-in or boneless)
- Turkey rub or seasoning blend
- Olive oil
- Wood pellets

Instructions:

1. Rub the turkey breast with olive oil and your chosen turkey rub or seasoning blend, covering it thoroughly.

2. Preheat your Traeger grill to 250°F (121°C) using cherry or pecan wood pellets for a fruity, nutty smoke flavor.

3. Place the seasoned turkey breast on the grill grates, skin side up.

4. Smoke the turkey breast for about 3-4 hours, or until the internal temperature reaches 165°F (74°C) for safe consumption.

5. Remove the smoked turkey breast from the grill and let it rest for 10-15 minutes before slicing and serving.

Portobello Mushrooms

Prep Time: 10 minutes | Cooking Time: 1-1.5 hours | Serves: 4

Ingredients:
- Portobello mushrooms, stems removed
- Balsamic vinegar
- Olive oil
- Garlic powder
- Fresh thyme leaves
- Salt and pepper
- Wood pellets

Instructions:

1. In a bowl, whisk together balsamic vinegar, olive oil, garlic powder, fresh thyme leaves, salt, and pepper.

2. Brush the portobello mushrooms with the balsamic mixture, coating both sides.

3. Preheat your Traeger grill to 225°F (107°C) using hickory or mesquite wood pellets for a smoky, robust flavor.

4. Place the marinated portobello mushrooms directly on the grill grates.

5. Smoke the mushrooms for about 1-1.5 hours, or until they are tender and infused with smoky flavor.

6. Remove from the grill and serve the smoked portobello mushrooms as a flavorful side dish or topping for salads and sandwiches.

Prime Rib Roast

Prep Time: 20 minutes | Cooking Time: 4-5 hours | Serves: 8-10

Ingredients:
- Prime rib roast (bone-in or boneless)
- Beef rub or seasoning blend
- Garlic cloves, minced
- Olive oil
- Wood pellets (hickory or oak recommended)

Instructions:
1. Rub the prime rib roast with minced garlic, olive oil, and your favorite beef rub or seasoning blend, ensuring even coverage.
2. Preheat your Traeger grill to 225°F (107°C) using hickory or oak wood pellets for a bold, smoky flavor.
3. Place the seasoned prime rib roast on the grill grates, fat side up.
4. Smoke the prime rib roast for about 4-5 hours, or until the internal temperature reaches your desired doneness (125°F for rare, 135°F for medium-rare).
5. Remove the roast from the grill and let it rest for 20-30 minutes before carving and serving.

Honey Glazed Ham

Prep Time: 15 minutes | Cooking Time: 2-3 hours | Serves: 10-12

Ingredients:
- Pre-cooked bone-in ham
- Honey
- Brown sugar
- Dijon mustard
- Cloves (optional for garnish)
- Wood pellets (apple or cherry recommended)

Instructions:
1. Score the surface of the pre-cooked ham in a diamond pattern.
2. In a bowl, mix honey, brown sugar, and Dijon mustard to create a glaze.
3. Preheat your Traeger grill to 250°F (121°C) using apple or cherry wood pellets for a sweet, fruity smoke flavor.
4. Place the ham on the grill and brush generously with the honey glaze.
5. Smoke the ham for about 2-3 hours, basting with the glaze every 30 minutes, until the glaze caramelizes and the ham is heated through.
6. Garnish with cloves if desired before serving.

Cranberry Stuffed Turkey

Prep Time: 30 minutes | Cooking Time: 12-15 minutes per pound | Serves: 12-14

Ingredients:
- Whole turkey, thawed
- Fresh cranberries
- Bread cubes
- Celery, chopped
- Onion, diced
- Poultry rub or seasoning blend
- Chicken broth
- Butter
- Wood pellets (maple or pecan recommended)

Instructions:
1. In a bowl, mix fresh cranberries, bread cubes, chopped celery, diced onion, and poultry rub or seasoning blend to create the stuffing.
2. Preheat your Traeger grill to 325°F (163°C) using maple or pecan wood pellets for a sweet and nutty smoke.
3. Stuff the thawed turkey cavity with the cranberry stuffing, securing with kitchen twine if necessary.
4. Rub the outside of the turkey with softened butter and additional poultry rub.
5. Place the stuffed turkey on the grill and roast/smoke for about 12-15 minutes per pound, or until the internal temperature reaches 165°F (74°C) in the thickest part of the thigh.
6. Let the turkey rest for 20-30 minutes before carving and serving with the delicious cranberry stuffing.

Cornish Hens with Herb Butter

Prep Time: 15 minutes | Cooking Time: 1-1.5 hours | Serves: 4

Ingredients:
- Cornish hens
- Herb butter
- Lemon slices
- Wood pellets

Instructions:
1. Rub the Cornish hens inside and out with herb butter, including under the skin for extra flavor.

2. Place lemon slices inside the cavities of the hens for additional aroma.

3. Preheat your Traeger grill to 350°F (175°C) using pecan or cherry wood pellets for a fruity smoke.

4. Arrange the herb-buttered Cornish hens on the grill grates.

5. Smoke the hens for about 1-1.5 hours, or until they reach an internal temperature of 165°F (74°C) and the skin is golden and crispy.

6. Remove from the grill and let them rest for a few minutes before serving as individual portions.

Smoked Pumpkin Pie

Prep Time: 15 minutes | Cooking Time: 50-60 minutes | Serves: 8

Ingredients:
- Pumpkin puree (canned or homemade)
- Eggs
- Evaporated milk
- Brown sugar
- Pumpkin pie spice (cinnamon, nutmeg, cloves)
- Pie crust (store-bought or homemade)
- Whipped cream (for serving)
- Wood pellets (maple or oak recommended)

Instructions:
1. In a bowl, whisk together pumpkin puree, eggs, evaporated milk, brown sugar, and pumpkin pie spice until smooth.

2. Pour the pumpkin mixture into a prepared pie crust in a pie dish.

3. Preheat your Traeger grill to 350°F (175°C) using maple or oak wood pellets for a rich smoke flavor.

4. Place the pumpkin pie on the grill and bake for about 50-60 minutes, or until the filling is set and the crust is golden brown.

5. Remove from the grill and let the pie cool completely before serving with whipped cream.

Appendix: Measurement Conversion Chart

VOLUME EQUIVALENTS (DRY)

US STANDARD	METRIC (APPROXIMATE)
1/8 teaspoon	0.5 mL
1/4 teaspoon	1 mL
1/2 teaspoon	2 mL
3/4 teaspoon	4 mL
1 teaspoon	5 mL
1 tablespoon	15 mL
1/4 cup	59 mL
1/2 cup	118 mL
3/4 cup	177 mL
1 cup	235 mL
2 cups	475 mL
3 cups	700 mL
4 cups	1 L

VOLUME EQUIVALENTS(LIQUID)

US STANDARD	US STANDARD (OUNCE)	METRIC (APPROXIMATE)
2 tablespoons	1 fl.oz.	30 mL
1/4 cup	2 fl.oz.	60 mL
1/2 cup	4 fl.oz.	120 mL
1 cup	8 fl.oz.	240 mL
1 1/2 cup	12 fl.oz.	355 mL
2 cups or 1 pint	16 fl.oz.	475 mL
4 cups or 1 quart	32 fl.oz.	1 L
1 gallon	128 fl.oz.	4 L

WEIGHT EQUIVALENTS

US STANDARD	METRIC (APPROXIMATE)
1 ounce	28 g
2 ounces	57 g
5 ounces	142 g
10 ounces	284 g
15 ounces	425 g
16 ounces / 1 lb.	454 g
32 ounces / 2 lb.	907 g
2.2 lb.	1kg

TEMPERATURES EQUIVALENTS

FAHRENHEIT(F)	CELSIUS(C)
225°F	107 °C
250°F	120 °C
275°F	135 °C
300°F	150 °C
325°F	160 °C
350°F	180 °C
375°F	190 °C
400°F	205°C
425°F	220°C
450°F	235 °C
475°F	245 °C
500°F	260 °C

Index

A

Almond Butter Cookies 91
Apple and Pecan Smoked Oat Crumble 21
Apple Crisp Bars 92
Applewood Smoked Turkey Bacon 15
Avocado and Egg Boats 20

B

Bacon-Wrapped Asparagus Bundles 31
Bacon-Wrapped Scallops 76
Banana Split Foil Packets 88
Barbecue Pulled Pork Breakfast Tacos 24
BBQ Chicken Wings 43
BBQ Meatloaf 60
BBQ Turkey Meatballs 47
Beef and Asparagus Roll-Ups 64
Beef and Black Bean Quesadillas 66
Beef and Mushroom Skewers 63
Beef and Pineapple Skewers with Teriyaki Glaze 65
Beef and Veggie Skewers with Chimichurri Sauce 61
Beef and Veggie Stir-Fry 64
Beef and Veggie Wraps with Avocado Sauce 66
Beef Brisket 94
Beef Kebabs with Vegetables 59
Beef Stuffed Portobello Mushrooms 65
Beef Tenderloin with Herb Butter 59
Beef Tenderloin with Red Wine Reduction 62
Blueberry Granola Crunch 16
Bourbon Pecan Pie Bars 92
Butternut Squash Soup 81

C

Caprese Stuffed Portobello Mushrooms 82
Cedar Plank Salmon 72
Charred Edamame 30
Chicken Alfredo Pasta 50
Chicken Alfredo Stuffed Peppers 51
Chicken and Spinach Stuffed Portobello Mushrooms 57
Chicken and Veggie Skewers 49
Chicken Caprese Salad 50
Chicken Pesto Flatbread 51
Chicken Teriyaki Rice Bowl 52
Chicken Tikka Masala 52
Chocolate Banana S'mores 87
Chocolate Chip Cookies 88
Chocolate Covered Strawberries 90
Cinnamon Apple Smoked Oatmeal 17
Cornish Game Hens with Rosemary Lemon Glaze 46
Cornish Hens with Herb Butter 98
Crab Cakes with Remoulade Sauce 74
Crab Legs with Garlic Butter 73

Crab-Stuffed Mushrooms 77
Cranberry Stuffed Turkey 98
Duck Breast with Orange Glaze 45
Duck Tacos with Mango Salsa 48

E

Eggplant and Chickpea Curry 83
Eggplant Caprese Salad 36

F

Fruit Salad with Honey-Lime Dressing 89

G

Greek Stuffed Portobello Mushrooms 83
Grilled Artichoke Hearts with Lemon Aioli 34
Grilled Avocado Boats 15
Grilled Avocado Stuffed with Quinoa Salad 37
Grilled Avocado Toast with Smoked Salmon 39
Grilled Avocado with Egg and Chorizo 25
Grilled Banana Bread 18
Grilled Breakfast Pizzas 22
Grilled Brie with Honey and Pecans 29
Grilled Bruschetta with Tomato and Basil 38
Grilled Cajun Shrimp Lettuce Wraps 34
Grilled Caprese Skewers 33
Grilled Cauliflower Steaks 81
Grilled Chicken and Asparagus Stir-Fry 55
Grilled Chicken and Avocado Sandwiches 55
Grilled Chicken and Pineapple Skewers 41
Grilled Chicken and Veggie Wraps 53
Grilled Chicken Caesar Pizza 45
Grilled Chicken Caesar Salad 43
Grilled Chicken Pita Pockets with Greek Salad 56
Grilled Chicken Satay Skewers with Peanut Sauce 32
Grilled Chicken Shawarma Wraps 54
Grilled Corn and Avocado Salad Cups 33
Grilled Corn and Avocado Salsa 28
Grilled Corn and Black Bean Salsa 38
Grilled Eggplant Parmesan 80
Grilled Flatbread with Pesto and Sun-Dried Tomatoes 33
Grilled French Croissant Sandwich 19
Grilled French Toast Kebabs 17
Grilled Grapefruit with Honey and Cinnamon 14
Grilled Halloumi and Veggie Skewers 40
Grilled Halloumi Cheese Skewers 39
Grilled Lemon Bars 90
Grilled Pancakes 16
Grilled Parmesan Garlic Artichokes 29
Grilled Peach and Yogurt Parfait 13
Grilled Peach Cobbler 89
Grilled Peaches and Cream French Toast 18
Grilled Peaches and Cream Oatmeal 26
Grilled Pineapple with Coconut Whipped Cream 87
Grilled Pita Bread with Herbed Yogurt Dip 34

Grilled Portobello Mushroom Burgers 80
Grilled Prosciutto-Wrapped Asparagus and Egg 26
Grilled Prosciutto-Wrapped Dates with Goat Cheese.......38
Grilled Prosciutto-Wrapped Pears 30
Grilled Sausage and Vegetable Hash 21
Grilled Shrimp and Pineapple Skewers 37
Grilled Snapper Veracruz 78
Grilled Stuffed Acorn Squash 81
Grilled Stuffed Baby Bell Peppers 39
Grilled Stuffed Calamari 77
Grilled Stuffed Jalapeños with Cream Cheese 41
Grilled Stuffed Mini Bell Peppers and Bacon..............34
Grilled Stuffed Mini Peppers 32
Grilled Stuffed Mushrooms 30
Grilled Stuffed Mushrooms with Herb Cheese............37
Grilled Stuffed Portobello Mushrooms 32
Grilled Sweet Potato and Kale Hash 24
Grilled Sweet Potato Nachos 40
Grilled Teriyaki Pineapple Chicken Skewers 33
Grilled Tomato and Spinach Benedict 20
Grilled Vegetable and Goat Cheese Frittata 23
Grilled Vegetable Quesadillas 35
Grilled Vegetable Skewers 80
Grilled Watermelon and Feta Skewers 38
Grilled Zucchini Roll-Ups 39

H

Halibut Steaks with Herb Butter 74
Halibut with Mango Salsa 72
Halloumi Cheese Skewers..30
Hash Brown Casserole..22
Hickory Smoked Breakfast Sausage............................14
Honey Garlic Glazed Chicken Drumsticks 45
Honey Glazed Ham 98
Honey Mustard Chicken Thighs 51
Honey Mustard Glazed Cornish Game Hens 47
Honey Sriracha Chicken Wings 36
Honey Sriracha Glazed Chicken Wings 49

K

Korean BBQ Beef Short Ribs..61
Korean BBQ Beef Tacos..63

L

Lamb Burgers with Feta and Tzatziki Sauce 68
Lamb Chops with Mint Chimichurri............................67
Lamb Gyros with Tzatziki Sauce..................................69
Lamb Kebabs with Yogurt Marinade............................67
Lamb Meatballs with Tomato Sauce............................68
Lamb Ribs with Spicy BBQ Glaze 68
Lamb Shanks with Red Wine Sauce............................69
Lamb Shoulder Chops with Garlic Herb Butter..........69
Lamb Shoulder with Herb Rub 68
Leg of Lamb with Rosemary Garlic Rub 67

Lemon Garlic Butter Shrimp Skewers 76
Lemon Garlic Chicken Kabobs....................................50
Lemon Garlic Chicken Wings 48
Lemon Herb Turkey Burgers 47
Lobster Mac and Cheese..77
Lobster Rolls 75
Lobster Tails with Garlic Herb Butter 71
Lobster Tails with Herb Citrus Butter 73

M

Mahi Mahi with Mango Salsa 73
Maple Glazed Chicken Drumsticks 48
Maple Glazed Duck Breast..43
Mussels with White Wine and Garlic..........................75

N

Nutella-Stuffed French Toast 89

O

Octopus with Chimichurri Sauce 78

P

Pancetta and Vegetable Frittata..................................20
Peach and Ricotta Grilled Toast 23
Pheasant with Herb Butter 46
Pineapple Upside-Down Cake 91
Pork Belly Burnt Ends 62
Pork Belly Tacos 65
Pork Carnitas Tacos 64
Pork Chops with Apple Compote 63
Pork Loin Chops with Maple Mustard Glaze..............67
Pork Loin Roast with Herb Crust 66
Pork Loin with Maple Glaze 63
Pork Ribs with BBQ Sauce 59
Pork Shoulder with Carolina Mustard Sauce 59
Pork Spare Ribs 66
Pork Tenderloin with Apple Glaze 61
Pork Tenderloin with Mustard Glaze..........................65
Portobello Mushroom Steaks 85
Portobello Mushrooms 96
Pound Cake with Berries and Whipped Cream 90
Prime Rib Roast..98
Prosciutto-Wrapped Asparagus 35
Prosciutto-Wrapped Dates..31
Prosciutto-Wrapped Pears with Goat Cheese 36
Pulled Beef Sandwiches 64
Pulled Pork Sandwiches 62

Q

Quinoa-Stuffed Bell Peppers 83

S

Salmon with Lemon Herb Butter 71
Scallops with Bacon Wrapped Asparagus 72

Shrimp Skewers with Garlic Butter 71
Shrimp Skewers with Lemon Garlic Butter 28
Shrimp Tacos with Pineapple Salsa 72
Smoked Apple Cinnamon Oatmeal 13
Smoked Apple Cinnamon Rolls 22
Smoked Apple Crisp 88
Smoked Banana Bread 90
Smoked Beef Ribs 95
Smoked Berry French Toast Casserole 25
Smoked Berry Oatmeal Crisp 25
Smoked Breakfast Hash 16
Smoked Breakfast Tacos 17
Smoked Cheese and Bacon Scones 24
Smoked Chicken and Corn Chowder 54
Smoked Chicken and Mushroom Risotto 53
Smoked Chicken Pesto Pasta 55
Smoked Chicken Quesadillas 49
Smoked Chicken Tacos with Mango Salsa 56
Smoked Chicken Thighs with Lemon Herb Butter 44
Smoked Chicken Wings with Honey Sriracha Glaze 32
Smoked Coconut Porridge 24
Smoked Cornish Hens 44
Smoked Deviled Eggs 29
Smoked French Toast Sticks 23
Smoked Gouda and Mushroom Crostini 28
Smoked Hash Browns 15
Smoked Maple Bacon Muffins 19
Smoked Oysters Rockefeller 78
Smoked Paprika and Garlic Grilled Shrimp 31
Smoked Peach Crisp 87
Smoked Pecan Pie 91
Smoked Pesto Chicken Thighs 47
Smoked Pork Belly Burnt Ends 95
Smoked Pork Shoulder (Pulled Pork) 94
Smoked Porridge with Mixed Berries 20
Smoked Pumpkin Pie 99
Smoked Quail with Cherry Glaze 46
Smoked Salmon and Asparagus Frittata 19
Smoked Salmon and Cream Cheese Bagels 13
Smoked Salmon and Cream Cheese Frittata 26
Smoked Salmon and Cucumber Bites 30
Smoked Salmon Bagel Platter 23
Smoked Salmon Dip 76
Smoked Salmon Frittata 16
Smoked Shakshuka 18
Smoked Stuffed Bell Peppers 80
Smoked Stuffed Jalapeños 28
Smoked Stuffed Peppers 95
Smoked Texas Turkey Breast 96
Smoked Turkey Breast 43
Smoked Vegetable Lasagna 81
Smoked Vegetarian Chili 95
Smoked Veggie Omelet 17
Smoked Whole Chicken 94

Smoky Bacon and Corn Pancakes 21
Smoky Breakfast Pizza 26
Smoky Chorizo and Egg Breakfast Burritos 22
Smoky Grilled Guacamole 29
Spinach and Ricotta Stuffed Portobello Mushrooms 82
Steak Fajitas 60
Strawberry Shortcake Skewers 87
Stuffed Acorn Squash with Wild Rice 85
Stuffed Bell Peppers with Quinoa 84
Stuffed Jalapeños with Cream Cheese and Bacon 35
Stuffed Mini Bell Peppers with Creamy Spinach 38
Stuffed Mini Potatoes with Bacon and Cheese 36
Stuffed Squid with Chorizo and Rice 74
Sweet Potato and Black Bean Enchiladas 84
Sweet Potato Fries with Chipotle Dip 35
Sweet Potato Tacos 82
Swordfish Steaks with Mediterranean Salsa 71
Swordfish Tacos with Chipotle Crema 74

T
Traeger Baked Blueberry Muffins 14
Traeger Breakfast Burgers 13
Traeger Grilled French Toast 14
Traeger Smoked Beef Brisket with Coffee Rub 64
Traeger Smoked Cheddar Biscuits 15
Traeger Smoked Cheese Grits 19
Traeger Smoked Chicken Enchiladas 53
Traeger Smoked Crepes 15
Traeger Smoked Salmon 94
Trout with Herb Butter 73
Tuna Nicoise Salad 76
Tuna Steaks with Sesame Soy Glaze 75
Turkey Burgers with Avocado Mayo 44
Turkey Meatloaf 50

V
Vegetable Paella 84

W
Watermelon with Mint and Feta 88

Y
Yogurt Parfaits 21

Z
Zucchini Rolls with Herbed Cream Cheese 31